W9-BWH-029

the supervision of the church, sometimes flirt with worldly ways and scorn the Ordnung. At baptism, however, young adults declare their Christian faith and vow to uphold the Ordnung for the rest of their life. Those who break their promise face excommunication and shunning. Those choosing not to be baptized may gradually drift away from the community but are welcome to return to their families without the stigma of shunning. Rooted in the Anabaptist tradition, baptism symbolizes the ultimate pledge to surrender one's life to the community of faith.

The drama of worship rehearsed in Amish homes reaffirms the essence of the Ordnung. Church districts hold services every other Sunday. A group of two hundred or more, including neighbors and relatives who have an "off Sunday," gather for worship. They meet in a farmhouse, the basement of a newer home, or a shed or barn—underscoring the integration of worship with daily life. A fellowship meal and informal visiting follow the three-hour service.

The plain and simple but unwritten liturgy revolves around a cappella singing and two sermons. Without the aid of organs, offerings, candles, crosses, robes, or flowers, members yield themselves to God in the spirit of humility. The congregation sings from the *Ausbund*—a hymnal of German songs without musical notations that dates back to the sixteenth-century Anabaptists. The tunes, passed across the generations by memory, are sung in unison. The slow, chantlike cadence creates a sixteenth-century mood. A single hymn may stretch over twenty minutes. Extemporaneous sermons, preached in the dialect, recount biblical stories as well as lessons from farm life. Preachers exhort members to be obedient to Amish ways.

Communion services, held each autumn and spring, frame the religious year. These ritual high points em-

phasize self-examination and spiritual rejuvenation. Sins are confessed, and members reaffirm their vow to uphold the Ordnung. Communion is held when the congregation is "at peace"—meaning that all members are in harmony with the Ordnung. The eight-hour communion service includes preaching, a light meal during the service, and the commemoration of Christ's death with bread and wine. Pairs of members wash each other's feet as the congregation sings. At the end of the communion service, members give an alms offering to the deacon—the only time that offerings are given in Amish services.

Baptism, worship, and communion are sacred rites that revitalize and preserve the Ordnung. But the Amish, like other human beings, forget, rebel, experiment, and stray into deviance. Major transgressions are confessed publicly in a "members' meeting" following the worship service. Violations of the Ordnung—using a tractor in the field, posing for a television camera, flying on a commercial airline, filing a lawsuit, joining a political organization, or opening a questionable business—are confessed publicly. Public confession diminishes self-will, reminds members of the supreme value of submission, restores the wayward into the community of faith, and underscores the lines of faithfulness that encircle the community.

The headstrong who spurn the advice of elders and refuse to confess their sin face a six-week probation. If their stubbornness does not mellow into repentance, they face excommunication. Exiles also face the *Meidung*, or shunning—a cultural equivalent of solitary confinement. Members terminate social interaction and financial transactions with the excommunicated. A bishop compared shunning to "the last dose of medicine that you give a sinner. It either works for life or death . . . but if love is lost, God's lost, too." For the unrepentant, social avoidance becomes a lifetime quarantine. An excommunicated member noted, "It works a little bit like an electric fence around a pasture."

The Meidung, a silent deterrent, encourages those who think about breaking their baptismal vows to think twice. The firm measures are taken to preserve the purity of the church and encourage repentance. Excommunicated members, even years later, can be restored into membership upon public confession of their sins. The use of shunning to preserve religious boundaries troubles tolerant modern minds. But even those who cherish tolerance are willing to expel unruly dissidents, political traitors, illegal aliens, and absentee employees.

The Riddle of Amish Survival

How does a traditional group flourish in the midst of modern life? At the turn of the twentieth century, Amish souls numbered some 5,000. Today their numbers exceed 130,000. Membership in some settlements doubles about every twenty years. What is their secret?

Three factors—biological *reproduction,* cultural *resistance,* and cultural *compromise*—have enabled the Amish to flourish in the modern world. The Amish do not actively evangelize. They do welcome outsiders, but few make the cultural leap. Growth is fueled by a robust birth rate that averages seven children per family. The dropout rate varies by settlement but usually dips below 20 percent. Thus, six out of seven children, on the average, remain Amish. But babies are not enough. Children must be persuaded to remain faithful to Amish ways.

The Amish have resisted the encroachment of modern culture by constructing social fences around their cultural turf. Core values are translated into visible symbols of identity. Badges of ethnicity—horse, buggy, lantern, dialect, and dress—draw sharp contours around Amish life. Daily use of these symbols reminds insider and outsider alike of the cultural divide between the two worlds. The Amish have resisted the forces of modernization in other ways as well. Cultural ties to the outside world are curbed by speaking the dialect, marrying within the group, spurning television, prohibiting higher education, and limiting social interaction with outsiders. Amish schools insulate their youth from the contaminating influence of worldly peers. Moreover, schools control the agenda of ideas. From birth to death, members are embedded in a web of ethnicity. These cultural defenses fortify Amish identity and help abate the lure of modernity.

Their survival strategy also involves cultural compromise. The Amish are not a calcified relic of bygone days, but are changing continually. Their willingness to compromise—to negotiate with modern life—often results in odd mixtures of tradition and progress. Tractors may be used at Amish barns but not in fields. Horses and mules pull modern farm machinery in some settlements. God smiles on electricity from batteries but not from public utility lines. Members frequently ride in cars or vans but aren't permitted to drive them. Telephones, found by farm lanes and shops, are missing from Amish homes. Modern gas appliances fill Amish kitchens in some states. And lanterns illuminate modern bathrooms in some Amish homes.

These riddles of Amish life often baffle, and appear silly, to outsiders. They reflect, however, delicate bargains that the Amish have struck between their desire to maintain tradition and the relentless press of progress. The Amish are willing to change, but not at the expense of communal values and ethnic identity. They use modern technology, but not when it disrupts family and community stability. Viewed within the context of Amish history, the negotiated compromises are reasonable, often ingenious ways of achieving community goals. Hardly foolish contradictions, they preserve core values while permitting selective modernization. They bolster Amish identity while reaping many benefits of modern life. Such flexibility boosts the economic vitality of the community and also retains the allegiance of Amish youth. Thus, in the final analysis, biological reproduction, cultural resistance, and cultural compromise have enabled the Amish to flourish as a distinctive people in the midst of the twentieth century.

This essay on the Old Order Amish of North America reflects the sentiments and values of virtually all the settlements. The photographs and vignettes in the remainder of this book, however, tell the story of the Amish community in Lancaster County, Pennsylvania. Lancaster's Amish share many religious values and social patterns with their Old Order cousins across North America, but the Lancaster Amish are less rural and more willing to use advanced technology than most Amish.

Lancaster's historic
Amish settlement
surrounds the small village
of Intercourse.

Washday on a typical
Amish homestead.
A community telephone
booth sits between the
hedge and the road.

The Old Order Amish of
Lancaster County

Lancaster County enjoys a fine reputation as one of the most productive agricultural communities in North America. Nestled in southeastern Pennsylvania, sixty miles west of Philadelphia, Lancaster's fertile acres face the steady press of urbanization. Indeed, the county has lost nearly 1,500 of some 6,000 farms since 1965. One of the fastest-growing counties in Pennsylvania, Lancaster gained over 100,000 people between 1970 and 1990 as its population swelled to 420,000. In the 1980s alone, the number of motor vehicles increased by 82,000.

Amish immigrants to the New World settled in neighboring Berks and Chester counties before coming to the Lancaster area about 1749. Several Amish congregations took root in Lancaster County during the nineteenth century, but they never flourished. Amish adults numbered fewer than 500 by 1900. The settlement prospered, however, in the twentieth century—doubling every twenty years as well as planting new colonies in other areas of Pennsylvania.

Lancaster's Old Order Amish community now exceeds 17,000 children and adults. Although Lancaster holds the distinction of being North America's oldest and most densely populated Amish settlement, Holmes County, Ohio, hosts the largest Amish community.

Sprawling to the east and south of Lancaster City, the settlement is organized into more than one hundred church districts—the fundamental social and religious units of the community. Some twenty-five to thirty family units constitute each church district of

Several generations often
live side by side.

165 persons on the average. Streams, fencerows, and roads form the boundaries of the various districts. The Amish own private property and live side by side with non-Amish neighbors on farms, along country roads, and in small villages.

U.S. Route 30 runs east and west through the county and divides the settlement physically as well as socially. Church districts south of this route have a higher proportion of farmers and tend to be more conservative religiously than their cousins to the north. Some fifty bishops give leadership to the religious life of the community, along with more than 250 ordained ministers and deacons.

The future of any society is uncertain, and so it is with the Amish. Ever encroached on by suburban de-

velopments, the Amish of Lancaster County offer an intriguing example of how a traditional religious group has coped with the pressures of modern life. Despite being the oldest settlement in North America, Lancaster's Amish have readily used modern technology. The saga of the Lancaster community is an interesting story in itself. But more importantly, it tells a tale of how other Amish communities may fare as they wrestle with the powerful forces of modernization. The fate of Lancaster's Amish may forecast the future of other Amish who refuse to flee from urbanization.

Winter marks the beginning and ending of seasonal cycles in Amish life. Mules tow a manure spreader on a snowy day in preparation for plowing.

Pupils trudge homeward across a field of corn fodder on a cold day.

A winter ice storm brings
both beauty and injury to
an apple orchard.

Plowing begins in late
winter as the soil begins to
thaw.

Ring-billed gulls follow the
plow in search of grubs
and worms.

Stewards of the Soil

Amish life is rooted in the soil. Ever since European persecution pushed them into rural areas, the Amish have been tillers of the soil—and good ones, too. The land has nurtured their common life and robust families. "It's been a longstanding tradition," said one leader, "that Amish families live on the farm, attached closely to the soil, and a good father provides a farm for his boys." In the words of another leader, "Good soil makes a strong church where we can live together, worship together, and work together."

But the rich limestone soil of Lancaster County is giving way to suburban sprawl and shopping malls. At the peak of loss in the mid-1980s, the county was losing nearly eight thousand acres of farmland a year. As urbanization devoured prime farmland, prices soared. Land in the heart of Lancaster's Amish settlement sold for $300 an acre in 1940. Today the same land sells for $8,000 to $10,000 an acre, even for agricultural use. The seventy-acre farm that brought $21,000 at midcentury may top $600,000 today. If a farm is sold for development, prices can double or even triple.

The shrinking farmland, coupled with the fact that the Amish population has doubled every twenty years, has created a crisis in the Amish soul. The community has coped with this crisis in several ways. Farms have been subdivided into smaller units with intensive cropping and larger concentrations of livestock. Some families have migrated to other counties in Pennsylvania and to the rural backwaters of other states in the Midwest and the South where farms can be purchased at much lower prices.

Lancaster's Amish have steadfastly spurned factory work—fearing it would fragment families and expose adults to cultural vices. Moreover, "lunch pail work" would untie the knots of communal dependency if members received insurance and other fringe benefits that flow from factory work. Squeezed off the land, deploring the factory, yet wanting to remain near ancestral homesteads, community leaders struck a deal with modernity. Yes, they would leave the land, but they would not trudge off to factories. They would create their own factories—small cottage industries anchored on Amish values.

In some church districts, a majority of families no longer till the soil. But those who have left their plows often worry about their children. Will more leisure and extra cash lead them astray? Even ex-farmers insist that the farm remains the best place to raise a family and hope that someday their children or grandchildren will return to the soil.

21

A horse-drawn rake awaits springtime use in the hayfields.

Two new twists illustrate the Amish struggle with the soil—the sale of some farms for development and the preservation of others. Over the years, the Amish have refused to sell farmland for development. Recently, however, several farmers have sold land to developers. Does this historic departure signal a new attitude toward the soil? Will the long-time stewards of the soil now sell it as a commodity? Historically, the Amish have shunned land preservation efforts, fearing they would lead to government entanglements. In 1991, the first Amish farms were preserved with Farmland Trust, a private preservation effort. This turn may enable some Amish land to withstand the forces of urban encroachment. These trends, in opposite directions, underscore the tenuous struggle with the soil.

A farmer drives a team of eight horses and mules to prepare the soil for seeding corn.

A team of five mules strains to pull a plow.

A community gathering at
an Amish schoolhouse
on a chilly March day.

Modern buildings on a
Lancaster County Amish
farm.

Man and beast work in
unison to prepare the soil
for springtime seeding.

A well-groomed draft
horse with a closely
trimmed mane.

Amish farms are often divided to cope with land pressures. New buildings on a subdivision are prepared for a barn raising.

Although modern tools are increasingly used, old-fashioned barn raisings remain an important means of mutual aid.

Non-Amish neighbors
sometimes assist with barn
raisings.

The *Ordnung* of the church prescribes clothing styles. Buttons, once forbidden, appear on coats at this public auction. Broadbrimmed black hats are typically worn in winter, and straw hats in summer. The mix of hats signals the changing seasons.

Understanding Social Change

Despite popular misconceptions, the Amish are not a fossilized relic of the past. The winds of change are blowing around the windmills that dot the Lancaster settlement. Although change often presses on them from the outside, it also is generated from within the community. How does it come about? Who draws the lines?

Economic pressures intensified by farming and business practices have spawned many changes. Others have come as families sought ease, comfort, and convenience within the boundaries of Amish society. The Ordnung regulates the rate of social change. Some practices, endorsed or forbidden by the Ordnung, become public flags of Amish identity.

The fifty bishops of the Lancaster settlement meet twice a year and, among other things, discuss troublesome changes. Innovations that pose little threat to the community or its identity are overlooked. Gas grills, for example, appeared on Amish patios in recent years. In other cases, the ordained leaders draw firm lines. Because the bishops feared they would lead to video games and television, computers were placed off-limits in 1986. Once embedded in the Ordnung, taboos are difficult to overturn. Sometimes new technology is accepted on top of old taboos—yielding a perplexing riddle. Many examples illustrate this ragged pattern of social change.

Power lawn mowers were forbidden in the fifties for fear they would bring ostentatious lawns and prideful hearts. Power mowers also threatened to steal work from Amish youth. A decade later, farmers were permitted to mount motors on field mowers. And still later, weed-eaters powered by bright red engines were deemed appropriate for lawns and gardens. Yet the taboo on power lawn mowers has held firm across the years. Thus, today, many homesteads sport old-fashioned push mowers alongside modern weed-eaters and power mowers in the fields.

Telephones and cars illustrate a similar pattern. Telephones were first barred from homes. Later they were permitted at the end of lanes and eventually adja-

A father writes a check for the purchase of equipment at an auction.

Power lawnmowers
are prohibited, but power
weed-eaters are often used.

cent to barns and shops and finally inside shops in some church districts. However, the original taboo on home phones has never fallen. Trying to respect the initial taboo, church leaders simultaneously yielded to pressure for business phones, resulting in a zigzag pattern of telephone use. A ragged pattern of change has also characterized car policies. The original proscription against *ownership* has held, while leaders have gradually permitted widespread *use* of vehicles to accommodate the need for greater mobility.

In short, practices that might erode traditional taboos or bring cultural contamination—microwave ovens, television, video games, video cameras, and computers—have little chance of being accepted. But other practices and products that pose no threat—

trampolines, hot dogs, and electronic calculators—slip into place with little fuss. And like any community, fads make their rounds here as well. Professional landscaping and the construction of outdoor decks, unheard of in earlier years, tantalize young Amish couples today.

A patchwork of social change results as elders try to retain traditional practices while yielding to new ones. Moreover, what is permitted varies by church district and the disposition of the local bishop. Collectively the bishops endeavor to uphold the historic markers of Amish identity ingrained in the Ordnung. But beneath the public markers, social change flows easily.

The crop rotation practiced by Amish farmers presents a symmetrical beauty.

Children assume significant responsibilities at an early age in Amish society.

Holstein cows are the breed of choice for Amish dairies.

Dairy Farming

Milk is the liquid gold of the Lancaster settlement. Until the middle of the twentieth century, the vast majority of Amish families engaged in diversified farming—tending small numbers of cows, hogs, chickens, and steers. Rising milk prices and the acceptance of bulk milk tanks led to specialized dairy farming in the sixties and seventies.

Amish farmers resisted the "worldly-looking" tanks whose refrigeration units required electricity from public power lines. They received a stark ultimatum in 1968 from milk companies: Install bulk tanks or lose your grade A milk markets. Following a series of meetings, Amish bishops and milk inspectors struck a deal. Yes, Amish farmers could install bulk tanks, but the refrigeration units must be powered by diesel engines, thus eliminating the use of public electricity. A critical turning point in Amish society, this decision held young families on the farm, boosted milk profits, and spurred the rise of specialized dairy farming.

Today automatic milkers suction the milk from forty cows in a typical Amish herd. Up-to-date veterinary services, vaccinations, medications, and commercial feed supplements enhance the productivity of Amish dairies. Farmers own registered, purebred dairy herds, but the church frowns on classifying cattle for show purposes. Many farmers participate in the Dairy Herd Improvement Association, use artificial insemination, and employ other state-of-the-art management techniques to improve milk production. However, embryonic transplants in dairy cows are discouraged by the church. Agricultural consultants advise some Amish farmers on the use of fertilizers, pesticides, and herbicides.

Although modern in many appearances, Amish farms do differ from non-Amish operations. Trying to

37

Milk inspectors regulate the sanitation of dairy barns. Typical herds have 40-50 cows.

Mechanical milkers are used by the Amish of Lancaster County. Diesel engines provide power for milkers and refrigeration tanks.

cap the size of dairy herds to keep them family operations, the Ordnung prohibits milking parlors, silo unloaders, automatic gutter cleaners, and glass pipelines for pumping milk from cows to tanks. These measures squeeze Amish herds to less than half the size of non-Amish ones. Although Amish farms are less automated than neighboring ones, feed and manure handling is often assisted by hydraulic or air-driven pumps and elevators.

Dairy farming leans heavily on alfalfa and corn. Cut four times throughout the summer, alfalfa is baled into hay for winter feeding. Fields of green corn—stalks and all—are chopped and blown into tall silos. Dried ear corn, picked in the fall, is ground for cattle feed. Leftover corn fodder is often baled for bedding.

Despite the automation, a sixty-acre dairy farm with forty cows and an assortment of thirty calves and heifers, as well as ten mules and horses, entails endless work. Some four hundred tons of green corn silage are cut in late August, hauled to the barn, and blown into silos for winter feeding. Moreover, one hundred tons of hay in the form of five thousand bales, as well as twenty tons of corn fodder, are baled in dusty fields, transported to the barn, and stacked in sultry storage mows. Approximately ninety tons of ear corn are picked and hauled to corn cribs for storage. Roughly two tons of feed are distributed to livestock each day in the winter. About one thousand pounds of milk are collected twice a day and transferred to the milk house. And, of course, there is manure—at least a ton a day in the winter months—to be flushed or scraped into thirty thousand-gallon holding tanks and eventually hauled to the fields. A typical farm with two-story buildings and some thirty thousand square feet under roof requires continual repair and maintenance, as does the farm equipment. All of this means that, despite the automation, farm work remains hard and dirty.

A mother and her newborn calf.

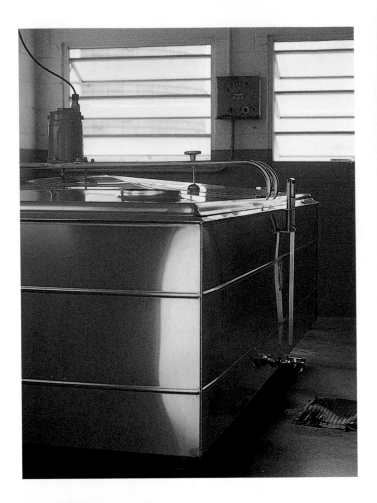

Milk is chilled and stored in bulk tanks.

A Brown Swiss cow. Her tag is number 18, but like every cow, she also has a name.

Several Amishmen
designed and manu-
factured this experimental
machine to compost
manure in order to reduce
barnyard run-off to nearby
streams.

A "honey wagon"
is used to haul and spread
manure.

A busy Amish homestead.
Grandparents live in the
apartment to the left of
the farmhouse.

Green corn is cut to make
silage for wintertime
feeding. A typical farmer
will store some 400 tons of
corn silage for a year's
feeding.

The Tractor Riddle

Tractors present another perplexing riddle of Amish life. Although they are standard equipment on Amish farms in Lancaster County, the tractors rarely venture into fields. Why are they used near barns but not in fields? This riddle, like many others, is rooted in history.

Tractors became available in the early 1920s after Amish leaders had banned the car. Some Amish farmers started using tractors in their fields, but elders worried that widespread use would eventually lead to the car. After all, farmers might drive tractors to town for supplies or even groceries. Over time, such habits would surely lead to the car. The early tractors, often awkward and expensive, were mockingly called "sod packers." This made it relatively easy for church leaders to recall them from Amish fields in the mid-twenties. Moreover, a progressive subgroup that left the Old Order Amish began using tractors. The tractor taboo helped to clinch the social boundaries between the two groups.

But there were other reasons to worry about using tractors in Amish fields. They would steal work from Amish boys. Unlike modern folks who are eager to save labor at every turn, the Amish welcome work as a wholesome way of keeping families together. Tethering tractors to the barn preserved field work for Amish lads. Factory work would pull families apart and place members in foreign cultural environments. Furthermore, relying on horses keeps farming operations small enough to be managed by one family. Tractors would trigger a spiraling cycle of bigness that mocks Amish values. And self-propelled equipment and other large implements would soon accompany trac-

tors. By keeping tractors out of fields, Amish leaders were able to limit the use of large equipment. Huge combines and forage harvesters would not only snatch work from Amish boys but also decimate the community crews that worked together at harvest time. In short, tractors and self-propelled equipment would wreak havoc on family and community life.

Moreover, horses and mules working in the fields helped to preserve a horse culture—the blacksmiths, harness makers, and carriage makers—scattered across Amish society. Widespread use of tractors might gradually erode horse and buggy travel altogether. Thus, over the years, the mules and horses plodding across fertile fields have carried the flag of Amish identity—marking off Amish turf with unquestionable clarity.

But why permit tractors at the barn? Why not eliminate the cancer completely? Since the late 1880s, Amish farmers had been using steam engines to power threshing machines. Small internal combustion engines had also powered wood saws, feed grinders, water pumps, and washing machines. Thus, when Amish elders restricted tractors to barn use they were, in essence, merely freezing history—using engines for extra power around the barn as they always had in the past.

Today modern tractors sit by Amish barns. They power feed grinders, spin ventilating fans, run manure pumps, operate hydraulic systems, and blow silage to the top of steep silos. This bargain serves the Amish well. Tied to the barn, tractors bring extra torque to dairy operations without threatening family or community life. Most importantly, the horse remains an unsullied symbol of Amish identity. Like many other riddles, this one strikes a delicate balance between tradition and technological progress.

Tractors are used
at the barn but not
in fields. This one powers
a cutter that chops and
blows green corn to the
top of a large silo.

Steel wheels are used on
tractors and other farm
equipment.

Amish farmers use
pesticides and herbicides.
Some farmers have
growing reservations about
the use of these chemicals.
Sprayers are manufactured
in Amish shops. This
farmer is spraying alfalfa.

A modern mower,
adapted for horses, cuts
alfalfa for hay.

A modern hay baler,
powered by a gasoline
engine, packs hay in tight
bales for storage.
Hay baling often requires
family cooperation.

The Riddles of Farm Machinery

Horses and mules pull modern machinery across Amish fields. This baffling marriage appears silly at first glance. If modern implements are permissible, why not pull them with tractors? The answer unfolds in the annals of Amish history.

When the Amish rejected the use of tractors for field work, horse-drawn implements were still easy to obtain. As non-Amish farmers replaced their horses with

tractors, horse-drawn equipment naturally dwindled. Faced with this sweeping change in farming, the Amish had several options: to manufacture their own horse-drawn implements; to convert tractor implements for horse use; or to take tractors to the field. Once entwined in the Ordnung, taboos are difficult to rescind, and the one prohibiting the use of tractors in the field held firm.

Economic forces also prodded the marriage between horses and modern equipment. Expanding dairy operations required more storage space for roughage. Hay balers, which became popular in the 1950s, enabled farmers to store hay in compact bales and boost dairy production without having to build larger barns. Several Amish farmers bought hay balers. By mounting an engine on the baler and supporting its weight with a forecart, a baler could be hitched to horses. This curious blend of tradition and progress charted a turning point in Amish farming. Soon other modern implements, powered by engines and towed by mules or horses, boosted the productivity of farming operations.

One leader, on reflection, said, "It surprises me that the baler slipped through." Searching for a rule of thumb to guide the changes, a senior bishop declared, "If you can pull it with horses, you can have it." This ingenious formula strikes a delicate balance. Modern machinery was welcome as long as it didn't retire the mules and horses. Moreover, sizable equipment was difficult to pull with animals. Despite the bow to progress, the horse—an enduring flag of Amish identity—would remain in the field, slowing things down and precluding the use of large equipment. But modern implements, pulled by mules and horses and now powered with gasoline engines, could provide the extra torque to harvest bountiful crops and hike milk production.

A young boy learns
from his brother how to
rake hay.

The bargain stuck. Over the years, a variety of new implements designed for tractors were adapted for horses by Amish mechanics. Gasoline engines appeared on grass mowers, corn pickers, roto beaters, and sprayers, among other implements. A productive compromise, it keeps the horse in the field and the family on the farm. It slows things down but also taps new power sources to harvest robust crops and boost productivity.

In recent years, the Amish have begun manufacturing some of their own farm equipment—plows, wagons, manure spreaders, sprayers, and corn planters. Today Amish farms sport a mixture of farm implements—hay balers, mowers, and corn pickers designed for tractors, but adapted for horses, as well as machinery manufactured in Amish shops. The colorful array, shaped by economic forces, blends traditional ways with modern feats in an interesting marriage that selectively harnesses the power of progress.

51

Children content themselves without expensive toys.

Hundreds of Amish
cottage industries produce
a diversity of products.

Cottage Industries

The rise of cottage industries marks a historic turn in the life of Lancaster's Amish community. These new enterprises, which mushroomed in the 1980s, have re-shaped the Amish landscape. Not only are the shops bold outward ventures, they also provide an internal network that channels social interaction within ethnic corridors. Joking about the array of new jobs, an old sage chimed, "About the only thing we don't have now is an undertaker." While not quite true, his quip sym-bolizes the booming growth of cottage industries. Re-tail shops sell dry goods, furniture, shoes, and whole-sale foods. Church members now work as carpenters, plumbers, painters, and self-trained accountants. Pro-fessionals—lawyers, physicians, and veterinarians—are, of course, missing from Amish ranks.

The new industries come in three forms. Home-based operations—lodged on farms or by new homes—employ a few family members and neighbors. Bake-shops, craft shops, hardware stores, health food stores, quilt shops, flower shops, and repair shops of all sorts are but a few of the hundreds of home-based opera-tions. Work in these settings revolves around the fam-ily. "What we're trying to do," said one proprietor, "is to keep the family together." A growing number of these small cottage industries cater to tourists, but many serve the needs of Amish and non-Amish neigh-bors alike.

Larger shops and manufacturing concerns are housed in newly constructed buildings on the edge of farms or on commercial plots. These formal shops, which have as many as fifteen employees, manufacture farm machinery, hydraulic equipment, storage barns, furniture, and cabinetry. Metal fabrication shops thrive on subcontracts with other manufacturers.

These larger industries are efficient and profitable. Low overhead, minimal advertising, austere management, modest wages, quality workmanship, and sheer hard work grant many shops a competitive edge in the marketplace.

Mobile work crews constitute a third type of industry. Amish construction groups travel to building sites in Lancaster County and surrounding areas. Nearly one hundred mobile crews have profited from the building boom in Lancaster County. The construction crews travel in hired vehicles and use the latest tools powered by portable generators and on-site electricity.

These new industries bear the imprint of Amish culture in several ways. They are, first of all, small. Church leaders fear that businesses with more than a dozen or so employees will bring pride, worldliness, excessive power, publicity—the evil trappings of large-scale operations. A smaller scale offers flexible work schedules to accommodate community activities—funerals, weddings, and special holidays. Small-scale operations harbor the dignity of work and pride in craftsmanship. Despite lacking professional training, the Amish nevertheless function as professionals by controlling the terms and conditions of their work.

The rise of cottage industries may, in the long run, disturb the equality of Amish life by encouraging a three-tier society—farmers, entrepreneurs, and day laborers. Will prosperous shopowners turn their profits back to the community or spend them on lavish lifestyles? Parents worry that youth, working a forty-hour week and with cash in their pockets, will snub traditional Amish values of simplicity and frugality. The new industries increase contact with the outside world. Such exchanges, over the generations, will surely prompt even more changes in Amish life.

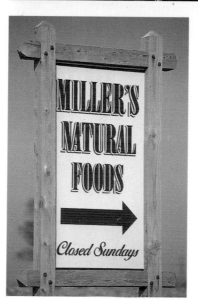

Amish society is patri-
archal. Farm auctions
provide a time for
informal consultation.

Selecting Leaders

Amish understandings of leadership diverge from modern ways. Ordained officials are literally called "servants" in German. Four officials, holding three roles, typically supervise a church district—a bishop (servant with full powers), two ministers (servant of the book), and a deacon (servant to the poor). Guided by the bishop, this leadership team directs the religious life of the community.

The selection of leaders mirrors Amish values and contrasts with modern modes of ordination. Amish persons neither seek office nor prepare for it through formal training. Aspiring for office is considered arrogant and haughty—a slap in the face of Amish humility. At baptism, male members agree to serve in leadership if called upon by the congregation.

Married men are eligible for office within their church district. Officials normally serve a life term. Character takes precedence over credentials in the selection process. Rather than highlighting competence or diplomas, the spotlight focuses on character, personal values, community esteem, and an embrace of Amish ways. Leaders earn their living by the sweat of their brow in their chosen occupation. They are not paid for services rendered but may receive occasional love gifts of food.

Leaders are selected and ordained by the congregation in a process known as "the lot," based on biblical precedents. The mysteries of divine selection guide the ritual. The ordination, held in a home, typically follows a communion service. Men or women may nominate males for the lot. Men who receive three or more votes are placed in the lot. Their baptismal promise makes it difficult to decline. Typically a half-dozen men may share the lot for minister. Ministers eventually become eligible for the office of bishop.

The lot "falls" on the new leader with little warning. A slip of paper bearing a Bible verse is hidden in a hymnbook. The book is mixed with other hymnbooks to equal the number of candidates. Each candidate selects a book. The officiating bishop says, "Lord of all generations, show us which one you have chosen among these brethren." As the books open and the fateful slip of paper appears, the lot "falls on the man as the Lord decrees."

The service swells with emotion. Like a bolt of lightening, the lot strikes the new minister and his family

Traditional hats and a full-grown beard are public symbols of identity for Amish men. Mustaches, associated in Amish folklore with European military officers, are forbidden.

55

Worship services are
held in homes or shops
every other Sunday. Men
and women enter from
separate entrances.

with the stunning realization that they will serve the congregation for the rest of their lives. Instead of congratulations and kudos, sobs of sympathy greet the family as they suddenly shoulder the burdens of servanthood.

Approximating a divine lottery to outsiders, this simple ritual serves the congregation well. Members can nominate the brightest and best, already intimately known in the circle of faith. The abrupt selection minimizes political campaigns and power plays. In the final analysis, the new leader is "chosen by the decree of the Lord." He may not be the first choice of some members, but his authority, legitimated by divine nod, surely supersedes that conferred by degrees and diplomas. Unhappy members can quarrel with God—not with a faulty political process. Moreover, only God fires Amish ministers. This simple, unpretentious ritual minimizes conflict, confers authority, and promotes stability in congregational life.

Children dressed in their
Sunday best.

Benches, songbooks, and
eating utensils are transported from home to
home for worship services.

Garden produce, fresh
and preserved, provides
food for families
throughout the year.

Amish families buy food,
often in bulk containers,
from both Amish and
non-Amish retail stores.

58

Bountiful Food

The bounty on Amish tables flows from a Pennsylvania Dutch culinary tradition shared with other groups in southeastern Pennsylvania. Food preferences among Lancaster's Amish vary by family and also somewhat by farm and nonfarm occupations. Although food lies beyond the reach of religious regulations, a traditional menu is typically served at large meals following church services, weddings, and funerals.

Breakfast fare for many families may include eggs, fried potatoes, toast, and commercial cereals such as cornflakes and Cheerios. Typical breakfast foods also include shoofly pie—sometimes dipped in, or covered with, coffee or milk—stewed crackers in warm milk, mush made from cornmeal, and sausage. Puddings and scrapple are also breakfast favorites. The puddings consist of ground liver, heart, and kidneys from pork and beef. These basic ingredients are also combined with flour and cornmeal to produce scrapple. The particular mix of these breakfast foods on an Amish table varies by season and family preference.

For farm families, the midday dinner is usually the largest meal of the day. Noontime dinners and evening suppers often include beef or chicken dishes, and vegetables in season from the family garden—peas, corn, green beans, lima beans, and carrots, to name a few. Mashed potatoes covered with beef gravy, noodles with brown butter, chicken pot pie, and sauerkraut are regional favorites. For side dishes and desserts there is applesauce, cornstarch pudding, tapioca, and fruit pies in season—apple, rhubarb, and pumpkin, as well as snitz pies made with dried apples.

Potato soup and chicken-corn-noodle soup are commonplace. In summer months, cold fruit soups—con-

sisting of strawberries, raspberries, or blueberries added to milk and bread cubes—appear on Amish tables. Meadow tea, homemade root beer, and instant drink mixes are used in the summer. Home-canned grape juice is a wintertime favorite.

Food preservation and preparation for large families and sizable gatherings is an enormous undertaking. Host families often bake three dozen pies for the noontime meal following the biweekly church service. Quantities of canned food vary, of course, by family size and preference. It is not uncommon for a family to can 150 quarts of applesauce, 100 quarts of peaches, 60 quarts of pears, 50 quarts of grape juice, and 50 quarts of pizza sauce, as well as the many other fruits, vegetables, and meats that are preserved in jars.

Although Amish tables are primarily supplied from family gardens, there are changes afoot. A growing proportion of food is being purchased from stores, sometimes operated by the Amish themselves. One Amishwoman estimates that only half of the families bake their own bread. The growing use of instant pudding, instant drinks, snack foods, and canned soups not only signals a tilt toward commercial food but reflects growing time constraints as well. The use of commercial food rises as families leave the farm and especially as women take on entrepreneurial roles. There are also economic considerations. A farmer's wife noted that "gardens are hardly worth the effort when you can buy canned fruits and vegetables in bulk so cheap."

Perhaps even more interesting is the arrival of ethnic foods. Homemade pizza is a favorite of many Lancaster Amish families. Pizza sauce made from homegrown tomatoes is canned in large quantities. Lasagna, stromboli, and yes, even taco salads and nacho chips are found on some Amish tables.

Cherries are picked in
July for table use and
canning.

Amish women typically
bake pies by the dozens.

Peaches are canned in a large vat over an open fire. Fruit and garden vegetables are canned in large quantities for winter months.

Shopping for
fabric at a retail store
operated by an Amish
woman.

Women Entrepreneurs

Recent changes in Lancaster's Amish community have opened occupational doors for Amish women. Although women have traditionally been tied to farm and homestead, some are now entering entrepreneurial roles. Single women have long worked as domestics and clerks in a variety of non-Amish settings. The emergence of Amish businesswomen, however, is a remarkable new turn in this patriarchal society. In recent years, these women have started an informal gathering to share ideas. Untouched by the winds of feminism, they are nevertheless flourishing in small businesses for a variety of reasons.

Declining farmland has pressed some families to search for new ways of earning a living. Flocks of tourists, hungry for Amish crafts, provide an easy and ready market. The booming interest in quilting provides a natural outlet for these traditional products. And the rise of hundreds of cottage industries has spurred Amish creativity and curiosity. Finally, church leaders have not impeded the flow of women into business roles.

Church leaders are typically not involved in a woman's decision to open a business. For a married woman, her husband's veto may be the biggest hurdle. Some of the new businesswomen are single, but others are grandmothers. Still others are mothers of young families. In all of these cases, women continue to hold household duties, although they are often assisted by many children.

Amish women operate a variety of businesses. Many tend small roadside stands on a seasonal basis in tan-

dem with household activities. They sell garden produce, crafts, canned fruits, jellies, and baked goods. Others manage permanent enterprises—clothing stores, food stores, bakery shops, flower shops, and tailor shops. One woman hosts a bed and breakfast operation. Another is self-employed as an artist. And quilt-making, of course, is big business. Quilting operations are sometimes divided into production stages at different locations. Entrepreneurs purchase quiltwork in various stages of completion from Amishwomen living in other counties as well as out of state. The women who manage these operations supervise the final quilting and sell the finished products to wholesale dealers or place them on the retail market.

Most women operate their business from their home or an adjacent office. Cottage industries typically involve the preparation and sale of products long associated with female roles—baked goods, garden produce,

63

A gasoline engine powers a mixer in a bakery shop operated by several Amish women.

Air or hydraulic pressure is sometimes used to power kitchen appliances. This Oster mixer is powered by air.

quilts, health foods, and clothing. These small commercial ventures embrace the value structure of Amish society—they are small, family-held, and family-operated. Such innovations serve the moral order of Amish society. It would be unthinkable, for example, for a woman to sell cosmetics, operate a video store, or open a styling salon.

But many things are new. Amish women, who have long deferred to their husbands to handle queries from outsiders, now freely interact with non-Amish suppliers, retailers, and customers. The entrepreneurs are developing commercial skills in marketing, accounting, labor relations, and management. And now they also enjoy a separate stream of income from their husbands—an independence unheard of in former days. These dual income arrangements will surely alter gender roles in years to come.

Women return from
market in a restored
spring wagon.

The Lines of Electricity

Electrical appliances—clothes dryers, hair dryers, air conditioners, dishwashers, VCRs, and TVs—are conspicuously missing from Amish homes. But electricity is used in other ways. Flashing red lights on buggies warn approaching traffic. Electric fences encircle cattle pastures. The elderly sometimes read by battery-powered lamps. Flashlights sit on household shelves. Carpentry crews use electrical power saws, and welding machines abound on Amish farms. What sort of logic underlies this maze of electrical lines?

The Amish church in Lancaster County forbade the use of public electricity as power lines were creeping into rural areas in the early 1920s. For folks who were trying to insulate themselves from the larger society, it made little sense to become hooked on the power of an evil world. Moreover, a progressive group that broke off from the Amish in 1910 began using electricity—a sure sign of its depravity. Fearing an unholy alliance with an evil world, asserting their self-sufficiency and steering away from the liberal group, the Old Order Amish turned their backs on public power.

The Amish had always used batteries to start motors and power flashlights. And so they simply continued to use batteries in old and new ways. As electricity permeated the larger society, a distinction gelled between 12-volt current (DC) stored in batteries and 110-volt current (AC) tapped from public lines. The Amish taboo on 110-volt current eliminated acrimonious debate over each new electrical gadget that flooded American homes in the twentieth century. As one Amishman noted, "Its not so much electricity that we're against, it's all the things that come with it—all the modern appliances, televisions, and computers. If we get electric lights, then where will we stop? The wheel of change would really start spinning then."

A variety of economic pressures have led to maverick uses of electricity. The installation of bulk milk tanks in 1968 brought the use of 12-volt agitators to stir the milk. In a clear break from the 12-volt tradition, church leaders in the 1960s permitted farmers to use electric welders, powered by portable generators, to repair farm machinery. Elders eventually permitted electric welders in Amish machine shops and the use of electric power tools by carpenters at construction sites.

Inverters have come into use in recent years. These small devices convert 12-volt current from batteries into 110-volt "homemade" electricity to operate cash registers, calculators, digital scales, and fans on sultry days. Twelve-volt motors operate a variety of small machines in Amish farms and shops. Some homes also use battery-operated appliances such as egg beaters.

The rejection of public electricity has shaped Amish identity over the years and etched a line of separation between Amish and modern worlds. Gas lanterns illuminate Amish homesteads, reminding insider and outsider alike of the boundaries of a different world. The intriguing compromises have enabled the Amish to tap electrical power to enhance business productivity, all the while paying deference to the historic taboo on public electricity.

Alternate Power

The taboo on 110-volt electricity crimped the productivity of Amish farms and shops. Because the taboo was central to Amish identity, Lancaster elders were reluctant to lift it. But how could Amish shops be powered without electricity? The question became urgent with the rise of cottage industries.

Amish mechanics soon discovered that large equipment could be operated by replacing electrical motors with hydraulic or air motors. Hydraulic and air pumps, powered by diesel engines, force oil or air through hoses to motors that spin grinders, saws, and other machines. Several Amish shops and mechanics specialize in converting equipment from electrical power to air and hydraulic. An unwritten rule quickly emerged: "If you can do it with air or oil, you may do it." Touting the success of "Amish electricity," one shop owner chortled, "We can do anything with air and hydraulic that you can do with electricity!" The productivity of Amish shops has soared with the aid of lathes, drills, sanders, and metal presses, to name only a few of the many machines now in use.

The shift to alternate power began at mid-twentieth century when Amish farmers used small gasoline engines to operate refrigeration units on their milk coolers. When bulk milk tanks arrived in the late 1960s, small diesel engines were used to power their refrigeration units. Diesel engines, now common on Amish farms, provide power for a variety of purposes.

Farmers tap air and hydraulic power to turn fans, power elevators, and operate feeders. Using an air celluloid, one farmer designed an automated system to

Diesel engines provide power for a variety of machines on Amish farms and in shops and homes. Air pumps and hydraulic pumps are powered by these engines.

67

feed his cows. An automatic timer triggered the feeding several times a day. Later he removed the timer, saying, "It was too worldly." Now he merely flicks a switch to feed the cows.

Many farmers pump their water with hydraulic power, speeding the demise of the windmill, longtime symbol of Amish farms. Air and hydraulic, pumped by diesel engines, ease work in many Amish households as well. Washing machines and occasionally cake mixers, food processors, and sewing machines run on "Amish electricity." Solar power is also sometimes used to charge batteries and power electric fences.

The use of alternate power enables selective modernization while still respecting the ban on public electricity. Air and hydraulic power symbolize Amish self-sufficiency, reinforce separation from the world, and mark a major feature of Amish identity. The use of alternate power is a creative and ingenious bargain that preserves tradition in the midst of progress. It remains culturally safe as long as radios, televisions, and computers cannot be run by air power. Some shop owners worry that they may fall behind as new equipment becomes more dependent on computer technology, which is forbidden by the Ordnung. For the moment, at least, "Amish electricity" has spurred vigorous economic growth without blurring the long-held lines of separation from the world.

Solar energy powers an
electric fence around an
Amish pasture.

An air gun and a hydraulic
lift are used to attach
shingles to the roof of a
gazebo manufactured by
an Amish cottage industry.

An Amish farmer drives a small tractor that he rented to do some grading around his home. The *Ordnung* of the church permits rubber tires on rented equipment.

A cattle feeder manufactured in an Amish machine shop. Electric welders are permitted in heavy equipment shops. Other modern tools are powered by air or hydraulic pressure.

This Amish shop
manufactures small
buildings for a variety of
purposes. Propane-
powered fork lifts, with
hard rubber tires, are
widely used.

An Amish home and
carriage shed. Newer Amish
homes appear strikingly
modern.

A flower bed.

This Black-Faced sheep sports contentment and well-being. Although the Amish buy synthetic fabrics for their clothing, a few farmers keep small flocks of sheep.

Father and daughter plow
the family garden.

The *Ordnung* permits
rubber tires on hand-
held items—wagons,
tricycles, small carts, and
wheelbarrows.

Health Care

Contrary to popular belief, the Amish do use modern medical services—to a certain extent. Lacking physicians within their ranks, they rely on the services of dentists, optometrists, and physicians based in health centers, clinics, and hospitals. They cite no biblical injunctions against modern health care nor the latest medicine, but they do believe that God is the ultimate healer. Despite the absence of religious taboos on health care, Amish practices do differ from prevailing patterns. Health habits also vary widely from family to family.

Compared to modern folks, the Amish are less likely to seek medical attention for minor aches or illness and more apt to follow folk remedies and drink herbal teas. Although they don't object to surgery or other forms of high-tech treatment, they rarely use heroic life-saving interventions. They are reluctant to quarrel with Mother Nature when their elderly face terminal illness. They are, in short, more willing to yield to the mysteries of Divine Providence.

In addition to using home remedies, church members often seek healing outside orthodox medical circles. The search for natural healing leads them to vitamins, homeopathic remedies, health foods, reflexologists, chiropractors, and the services of specialized clinics in faraway places. These cultural habits are shaped by many factors—conservative rural values, a preference for natural antidotes, a lack of information, a sense of awkwardness in high-tech settings, and the lack of accessible health care, as well as a willingness to suffer and to lean on the providence of God.

Children can attend Amish schools without immunizations. However, the community has no religious scruples against vaccinations. Some parents follow the advice of family doctors or trained midwives and immunize their children, but many don't. The failure to immunize is often due to cost, distance, misinformation, or lack of interest. Occasional outbreaks of German measles, whooping cough, polio, and other contagious diseases prompt public health campaigns to immunize Amish children. Amish elders usually encourage their people to cooperate with such efforts. In recent years, a variety of health providers have made special efforts to immunize Amish children.

Marriages within stable geographical communities and the influx of few converts restrict the genetic pool of Amish society. Marriages sometimes occur between second cousins. Such intermarriage, however, does not necessarily produce medical problems. But when unique recessive traits are common in a closed community, certain diseases are simply more likely to occur. On the other hand, a restricted gene pool may protect the Amish from other hereditary diseases.

A special type of dwarfism accompanied by other congenital problems occurs at an exceptionally high rate in the Lancaster settlement. Higher rates of deafness have also been found. In the late 1980s, Dr. Holmes Morton identified the presence of glutaric aciduria in Lancaster's Amish community. This disease, formerly unrecognized in the community and untreatable, is a biochemical disorder with symptoms similar to cerebral palsy. Approximately one in two hundred Amish infants inherits the disease. By 1991, Dr. Morton had organized a special clinic that tested some 70 percent of Amish infants and treated those diagnosed with the disease. In a cooperative venture of hope, the Amish community joined hands with many other friends to establish the clinic, which will surely boost health care within the community.

Amish farmers practice
crop rotation and contour
farming.

The Politics of Separation

The Amish view government with ambivalence. Although they support and respect civil government, they also keep a healthy distance from it. On the one hand, they follow biblical admonitions to obey and pray for rulers. Church leaders encourage members to be law-abiding citizens. On the other hand, government epitomizes worldly culture and the use of force. European persecutors of the Anabaptists were often government officials. Moreover, when push comes to shove, governments engage in warfare, use capital punishment, and impose their will with raw coercion. Believing that coercion mocks the gentle spirit of Jesus, the Amish reject the use of force, including litigation. Since they regulate many of their own affairs, they have less need for outside restrictions.

When civil law and religious conscience collide, the Amish are not afraid to take a stand and obey God rather than man, even if it brings imprisonment. On numerous occasions in the twentieth century, Lancaster's Amish have sat in prison for violating school regulations that rankled their conscience. They have clashed with government officials over the use of hard hats, zoning regulations, workers' compensation, and building codes for schools. As conscientious objectors they have enjoyed freedom from military service. Many received farm deferments or served in alternative service programs when the military draft was in effect.

The church has forbidden membership in political organizations and the holding of public office. (Serving as a public school director was permitted before the rise of Amish schools.) Holding political office is objectionable for several reasons. First, running for office is

Amish and non-Amish gather outside a polling place. Amish voting often increases when land use and zoning become heated issues.

viewed as arrogant, as out of character with the Amish values of humility and modesty. Second, office holding violates the religious principle of separation from the world. Finally, public officials must be prepared to use legal force if necessary to settle civic disputes. The exercise of legal force mocks the meek stance of nonresistance. In all of these ways, seeking, holding, and promoting political office contradicts Gelassenheit—the spirit of humility.

Voting, however, is viewed as a personal matter. The church has never prohibited it. Those who do vote are likely to be younger businessmen concerned about local issues. Thus, members are more likely to cast ballots in local elections than in national ones. One member esti-

mated that "only about 15 percent of the men vote unless there's a hot local issue." Discussing an upcoming primary election, one Amishman indicated that "the Amish vote" would support a township supervisor espousing land preservation. Although voting is considered a personal matter, jury duty is off limits. Joining political parties, attending political conventions, and campaigning for candidates flies in the face of Amish virtues—simplicity, humility, and separation from the world. Moreover, the deliberate use of force, often required in political life, contradicts the Amish spirit.

Children, dressed in the
garb of their parents,
enjoy a lighter moment.

A scarecrow outfitted in
Amish clothing guards a
cherry tree.

Children enjoy
bouncing on a trampoline,
a common form of
recreation.

Leisure

Leisure and pleasure have long been suspect in Amish life. Idleness is viewed as the devil's workshop. But the rise of cottage industries and more ready cash has prompted recreational activities. Said one Amish entrepreneur, "We're business people now, not just backwoods farmers, and sometimes we just need to get away from things."

The new recreational ventures remain, for the most part, entrenched in Amish values. Group oriented, they tilt more toward nature and travel than commercial entertainment. The Lancaster Amish rarely take "vacations," but they do take "trips" to other settlements, which often involve side trips to scenic sites such as the Skyline Drive in the Shenandoah Valley of Virginia. Groups often travel by chartered bus or van to other settlements for reunions, special gatherings, historical tours, or even to a state park or city zoo. Buses and vans also transport volunteer crews to disaster areas, where they marry leisure with goodwill as they clean up and rebuild after floods, tornadoes, or hurricanes.

Among youth, seasonal athletics are common—softball, sledding, skating, hockey, and swimming. Volleyball is a widespread favorite. Some youth play tennis and racquetball. Pressing beyond farm ponds and nearby streams, some youth travel to the beach for a summer splash.

Fishing and hunting for small game are favorite sports on farms and in woodlands. In recent years, some Amishmen have purchased hunting cabins in other counties of Pennsylvania, where they hunt white-tailed deer and enjoy a reprieve from home. Deep-sea fishing trips are common summertime jaunts for men. Others prefer camping and canoeing. Pitching quoits is common at family reunions and picnics. One farmer constructed a makeshift putting green in his pasture to practice golf strokes on the sly. Racquetball and golf, however, are rare exceptions.

Some couples travel to Florida for several weeks over the winter and live in an Amish village in Sarasota populated by winter travelers from settlements in several states. Trips to distant sites in search of special medical care sometimes include scenic tours as well. Although some folks travel by train or bus, chartered vans are by far the popular mode. Traveling together with family, friends, and extended kin, these mobile groups enjoy the laughter and chatter that bonds and builds community life.

83

Sporting colorful lunch pails, pupils head homeward.

Schools and Scholars

"We're not opposed to education," said one Amishman, "we're just against education higher than our heads; I mean education that we don't need." Indeed, the Amish supported public education when it revolved around one-room schools in the first half of the twentieth century. Under local control, the one-room rural schools posed little threat to Amish values. The massive consolidation of public schools and growing pressure to attend high school sparked clashes between Lancaster's Amish and state officials at midcentury.

Amish parents refused to turn their offspring over to the state. They weren't about to bus their youth off to faraway schools, nor were they eager to have strange subjects taught by strange teachers with little sympathy for Amish values. Confrontations in Pennsylvania and several other states led to arrests and brief stints in jail.

One-room Amish schools sprang up around Lancaster and in many other settlements as consolidation efforts rippled across the country. After legal skirmishes in several states, the U.S. Supreme Court gave its blessing to the eighth-grade Amish school system in 1972, saying, "There can be no assumption that today's majority is 'right' and the Amish and others are 'wrong.'" The court concluded that "a way of life that is odd or even erratic but interferes with no rights or interests of others is not to be condemned because it is different."

Some thirty to thirty-five "scholars" fill eight grades in Amish one-room schools. A Scripture reading and prayer open each day, but religion is not formally taught in the school or in other Amish settings, for that matter. The curriculum includes reading, arithmetic, spelling, grammar, penmanship, history, and some geography. Both English and German are taught. Because children have been nurtured in the Pennsylvania

85

One-room Amish schools accommodate eight grades.

German dialect, the classroom provides the first exposure to English for some of them. Parents want children to learn German to enhance their ability to read religious writings, many of which are in formal German. Science and sex education are missing, as are the other typical trappings of public schools—sports, dances, cafeterias, clubs, bands, choruses, computers, television, teacher strikes, guidance counselors, principals, and college recruiters.

A local board of three to five fathers organizes the school, hires a teacher, approves the curriculum, oversees the budget, and supervises maintenance. Teachers receive about $25 to $35 per day. The cost per child is roughly $250 per year—nearly sixteen times lower than nearby public schools, where per pupil costs often top $4,000. Amish parents pay public school taxes as well as their own. In one Lancaster church district, adult members pay an annual head tax of $120 to support their Amish school, as well as $120 per scholar if they are parents.

Schools play a critical role in the preservation of Amish culture. They not only reinforce Amish values but also shield youth from contaminating ideas. Moreover, schools restrict friendships with non-Amish peers and impede the flow of Amish youth into higher education and professional life. Amish schools harbor the young within the confines of an Amish world as they step toward adulthood.

Amish schools promote practical skills to prepare their graduates for success in Amish society. Some selective testing indicates that Amish pupils compare favorably with rural peers in public schools on standardized tests of basic skills. But do they prepare Amish youth for meaningful lives in Amish society? That, in essence, is the key question. The answer is surely yes. These islands of parochialism also teach cooperation, responsibility, hard work, and persistence, which ably serve both those who stay and those who leave the Amish faith.

Pupils practice for a
parent's day program.

Teachers

On the last day of school, a first grader walks to school early. She bursts into the classroom with a smile and runs up to her teacher. "These are for you," she beams, handing her a bouquet of daffodils. "I picked them down by the stream." Other pupils bring their own last-day gifts—needlework, baked goods, crafts, and wood-

A teacher assists a student
on an art project.

work. These fruits of love flow from youthful hearts on a May morning. "I'm not in this for the money," said one teacher. "There are deeper rewards—smiles of pleasure at a parent's program, an evening with a family, a birthday celebration, and an invitation to a wedding—these are the things that make it worthwhile."

Amish teachers, trained in Amish schools, are not certified by state officials. The brightest and best of Amish scholars, they return to the classroom to teach, often in their late teens and early twenties. Amish school directors select them for their ability to teach, commitment to Amish values, and availability. They are frequently single women, and they typically stop teaching if they marry. Without the benefit of high school or college diplomas they manage some thirty pupils across eight grades. Periodic meetings with other teachers, a monthly teachers' magazine, and ample common sense support their efforts.

Ironically, although Amish teachers lack professional training, they enjoy a remarkable amount of professional freedom. Without principals, department heads, or curriculum committees, they freely use their best judgment to establish classroom routines, standards of discipline, teaching methods, and the academic curriculum. Some textbooks are recycled from public schools, while others are produced by Amish publishers.

With three or four pupils per grade, teachers often teach two grades at a time. Pupils in other classes ponder assignments or, as the case may be, listen to previews of next year's lessons or hear reviews of past work. Classrooms exhibit a distinct sense of order amidst a beehive of activity. Hands raise to ask permission or clarify instructions as the teacher moves from cluster to cluster teaching new material every ten or fif-

Teachers are often young single women.

teen minutes. Students receive a remarkable amount of personal attention despite the teacher's responsibility for eight grades. Surprised by the orderly vitality of an Amish classroom, a first-time observer said, "This is the way things are supposed to be."

The ethos of the classroom accents cooperative activity, obedience, respect, diligence, kindness, and the natural world. Little attention is given to independent thinking and critical analysis—the esteemed values of public education. Despite the emphasis on order, playful pranks and giggles are commonplace. Schoolyard play in daily recesses often involves softball or other homespun games.

Amish schools exhibit a social continuity rarely found in public education. With many families sending several children to a school, teachers may relate to as few as a dozen households. Teachers know parents personally as well as the special circumstances surrounding each child. Children, in some cases, have the same teacher for all eight grades. Indeed, all the children from a family may have the same teacher. Such integration eclipses modern education, where students breeze by dozens of teachers, and the teachers, in turn, instruct pupils from hundreds of families. Amish schools are unquestionably provincial by modern standards. Yet, in a humane fashion they ably prepare Amish youth for meaningful lives in Amish society.

Classes are sometimes
held outdoors in pleasant
weather.

Schools are typically
located at the edge of a
farm. Land is often
donated by a parent.

Tobacco seedlings are transplanted to fields in June.

Tobacco

Why do the Amish raise and smoke tobacco? With religious taboos on other behaviors, why not one on tobacco as well? King of the cash crops, tobacco has flourished in Lancaster County since Civil War days. Virtually all farmers—Amish and non-Amish alike—formerly planted several acres of it. A favorable climate and rich soil produced bountiful crops of cigar filler and, later, cigarette tobacco. Labor-intensive tobacco farming provided ample work for family members, not only throughout the summer, but in winter months as well. Moreover, in the words of one Amishman, "Tobacco was the best mortgage lifter around." When prices are strong, tobacco may yield a profit of $2,500 per acre.

Between 1960 and 1980, tobacco acreage plummeted from 28,000 to 12,000 in Lancaster County. Several factors tarnished tobacco's glory. Milk prices were on the rise as tobacco prices skidded. Public health warnings about the hazards of smoking were also growing. Besides, tobacco harvesting had not been mechanized like other farm functions. Thus, in the 1960s and 1970s Amish and non-Amish farmers alike retired their tobacco spears and added more cows.

About one-half of the Amish farmers across the Lancaster settlement still raise several acres of tobacco. Alfalfa and corn, however, reign supreme over the farmland because they support the dairy operations. A dip in milk prices and a rise in tobacco values in the early nineties enticed some farmers to plant tobacco once again; but despite yearly fluctuations, tobacco's glory days are probably gone.

Raising and using tobacco was always considered an individual decision, since it posed little threat to the

A father drives while two
sons hand-plant and water
tobacco seedlings.

welfare of the community. Until the middle of the twentieth century, tobacco raising and use, a bedrock of rural life, was simply passed from generation to generation by Lancaster farmers of all religious stripes. Tobacco raising reinforced Amish commitments to family and to work. It steered Amish youth away from the devil's workshop of idleness. More importantly, it deterred them from factory jobs. Tobacco also pulled Amish families together. Grandparents and grandchildren labored together in the tobacco fields of summer as well as in the stripping rooms of winter. The lure of a profitable cash crop as well as the affirmation of family and work reflected basic Amish values.

Although Amish opinions vary on the use of tobacco, the church has never viewed it as a moral issue. No biblical teachings prohibit it. Furthermore, it poses few threats to community life. Perhaps a third of

Amishmen smoke cigars, pipes, or brown-wrapped cigarettes. Commercial white-wrapped cigarettes, however, are frowned upon as "too worldly."

A long-established custom in a peasant culture, smoking was commonly accepted as an everyday habit of personal choice. Cut off from mass media (especially television), scientific studies, and high school health classes, the Amish are less aware of the hazards associated with smoking. Nevertheless, as many members learn of its dangers, smoking is dwindling. In the words of one Amishman, "Smoking among our people has declined drastically in the last ten years." Some leaders discourage smoking, but others see little harm in it. Farmers who enjoy smoking are not troubled, of course, by raising tobacco. And in a peasant culture that values tradition and downplays independent, critical thinking, even some nonsmokers have few moral qualms about raising it.

Tobacco stalks are cut and speared on wooden laths in August.

A wagon transports tobacco from fields to drying sheds.

Tobacco is hung in
ventilated sheds to dry.
In winter months the
leaves are stripped off in
the cellar of the shed,
bound in bales, and sold
at auction.

Tobacco leaves curing in
the fall.

A neighbor offers her
son to help with milking,
asking, "Is Jake gonna
make hay tonight?"

Childbirth

Upwards of 60 percent of Lancaster's Amish babies
greet this world at home under the supervision of certified non-Amish midwives. Other children in the Lancaster settlement make their debut in birth centers,
hospitals, or clinics adjoining a doctor's office. Some
mothers prefer a hospital setting for their first birth but
then stay home for later births. In the 1950s and 1960s,
most Amish children were born in hospital delivery
rooms. The availability of licensed midwives and rising
hospital costs encouraged home deliveries in the late
1970s. Moreover, home deliveries fit the contours of
Amish values—local, familial, natural, simple, and
self-sufficient.

Certified nurse midwives who deliver babies at home
urge Amish parents to take childbirth classes. According to one midwife, "Ninety-nine percent of first-time
mothers and fathers take the classes." In addition to su-
pervising deliveries, the midwives also offer postpartum care and make home care visits six weeks after delivery. Many families share the bounty of their gardens
and ovens with midwives as a special thank-you for
home care services. The tab for a home delivery—
including prenatal and postpartum services—is approximately $1,000 for the first child and somewhat
less for later ones. Hospital deliveries range from
$2,500 for a typical birth to upwards of $5,000 for a
Cesarean section. A midwife estimates the rate of Cesarean sections among Amish mothers at 5 percent or
less—quite low compared to rates of nearly 25 percent
in local hospitals. Several physicians provide backup
services for midwives and birth centers in the event of
special complications.

Two relatives often come to assist in a household at the time of delivery. One stays with the mother and baby for three or four days, and the other runs the household for two weeks. A physician who delivers Amish babies beyond hospital walls notes, "Amish women are confident about birthing. They know what they're doing. There's always a grandmother nearby to help out." A midwife agreed, "They are comfortable with birthing and breast-feeding. They are surrounded by mothers, grandmothers, and older sisters. They see mothering all the time. It's just a normal part of their environment. They are comfortable with labor. I rarely get any requests for pain medication." Virtually all the mothers delivering at home and many of those delivering at hospitals breast-feed their babies.

And what of Amish fathers? Usually nearby, they assist with the birth as needed. "I do have trouble getting fathers to help when it's milking time," said a midwife, "but as a whole they are attentive, sensitive, and very supportive. The farmers are familiar with animal births, and so the whole process doesn't gross them out."

Artificial means of birth control are rarely used. Natural family planning and breast-feeding help to space the children, which average about seven per family. "I don't have many families with under six children," noted a midwife, "and some have eight to twelve." Although church officials frown on artificial birth control, a few couples may quietly use artificial means to limit family size. Some older women undergo tubal ligations because of medical complications or to terminate childbearing. As in other areas of Amish life, couples are urged, whenever possible, to yield to the mysteries of Mother Nature.

An ear of corn becomes a
homemade toy.

Dresses vary in color but lack prints and designs. They are typically fastened with straight pins.

Amish women often express their creativity in colorful flower gardens.

An outdoor telephone
booth shared by several
families sits beside a
public road.

The Telephone Puzzle

"Telephones," said one grandmother, "are still on probation." The Lancaster Amish use them selectively. Forbidden inside homes, telephones are often found near shops and barns or in "shanties" by a public road. Why would such an indispensable modern tool pose problems for Amish life? Although it is puzzling to outsiders, the telephone mystery begins to unfold in historical context.

Telephones entered American homes in the first decade of the twentieth century. A few Amish families installed them in the early days, but phones soon became prominent symbols of "worldliness." They were banned from Old Order Amish homes about 1910. The formation of a progressive subgroup of Amish dissidents helped to clinch the decision. Upon leaving the Old Order church, they started using the phone, turning it into a symbolic divider between the two groups. But there were deeper reasons why the Old Order Amish were hedging on the phone.

The telephone linked rural folks to the outside world. Devoid of cars, radios, electricity, and even reliable mail service, rural communities were quite isolated at the turn of the century. For the Amish, who hoped to remain separate from the larger society, the telephone tied them directly to the outside world. Strangers could freely enter Amish homes via the telephone. Besides, a ringing phone disrupted the natural flow of family living—allowing outsiders to interrupt things at any moment.

Moreover, face-to-face interaction and spontaneous visiting bond the members of Amish society together. If one can call, why visit? Telephones extract conversations from their contextual setting of body language, dress, hair, facial expression, and eye contact. These subtle clues signal religious meanings in Amish society.

In this sense, phone conversations are "half messages" stripped of body language and other rich contextual symbols. Furthermore, in contrast to face-to-face conversation, phone talk is more formal, abstract, distant, and mechanical.

Apart from the tag of "worldliness," no other religious injunctions were cited against the phone. Its *use* was never forbidden. In the early decades of the twentieth century, Amish persons often "borrowed" phones in neighboring homes or public places. By midcentury, however, some members pleaded for telephones to call veterinarians, place feed orders, make appointments, and handle emergencies. Moreover, it was embarrassing to drag barn dirt and smells into the homes of non-Amish neighbors.

By midcentury, church leaders finally agreed to permit telephone "shanties" at the end of farm lanes. Such phones were primarily used for outgoing, rather than incoming, calls. Furthermore, they were "community phones"—shared by several families. Telephone shanties proliferated after 1960. As the number of Amish cottage industries spiraled upward in the 1980s, the telephone became necessary for ordering supplies and selling products. In many cases, phones were installed in shanties near Amish shops. Although phones are still banned inside homes, their installation in shops and other outbuildings varies considerably by church district.

The taboo on home phones has, over the years, become a symbolic marker of Amish identity. Selective use of telephones is a way of mastering technology—using it without becoming enslaved to it. The telephone compromise is yet another way of absorbing change—flexing with financial and social needs—while still honoring tradition and preserving Amish identity.

A bottled-gas container
(*far right*) is one
identifying mark of both
older and newer Amish
homes.

Newer Amish homes have contemporary kitchens with gas stoves, refrigerators, and water heaters. Diesel engines often provide power to pump water.

A lantern hangs in the dining room of a newer Amish home. Open areas enable 150 people or more to gather in a home for worship services.

The bedroom of a teen-age boy.

Sowing Wild Oats

The late teenage years are an ambiguous stage in Amish life. Like other youth, the Amish swing between the innocence of childhood and the responsibilities of adult life. Amish youth, however, bypass high school and college and spend little time "finding themselves" as they move from adolescence into adulthood.

The Amish church places supreme importance on adult baptism. Those who take the vow commit themselves to Amish ways—the Ordnung of the church—for life. Unrepentant backsliders face excommunication and shunning. The decision to join the church is *the* decision for Amish youth. Young folks typically kneel for baptism between sixteen and twenty-two years of age. Women are often baptized younger than men. Since only church members can be married, young men sometimes kneel for baptism in the autumn before their wedding.

Prior to baptism, youth are outside the jurisdiction of the church. The alley of freedom between childhood and baptism affords those with a rebellious heart a chance to sow wild oats. The last chance for freedom before accepting the harness of the Ordnung, the late teen years offer an opportunity to test the boundaries of Amish turf and explore the outside world.

Amish teens often join one of a dozen or so youth groups that crisscross the settlement. Each group of one hundred to two hundred members has its own name—Antiques, Pilgrims, Quakers. The groups often gather for supper and a singing at a member's home on Sunday evenings. They often play volleyball in seasonable weather and toss darts or compete in Ping-Pong in winter months. Members also play softball and go skating and hiking.

A few rebellious groups sometimes snub Amish virtues. Members of these crowds own cars, attend movies, or venture to the city or the beach for a weekend fling. The more rebellious groups sometimes host parties— "hoedowns"—that are held in barns. The parties, with some use and abuse of alcohol, occasionally lead to arrests. Such activities embarrass church leaders and pain the hearts of parents. Despite these flirtations with worldliness, four out of five youth eventually join the church.

The freedom to sow wild oats gives youth the impression that church membership is a choice. Indeed it is. Some seek other paths, but for the most part the forces of Amish life funnel youth toward baptism in powerful ways. Beyond the web of family, friends, and school, romantic ties and economic incentives also pull youth homeward. The freedom of the teenage years creates an illusion of choice. But the perception of having a choice encourages adults to uphold the Ordnung in later life. After all, they had a chance to explore the outside world and count the cost of membership before joining the church. Such thinking bolsters adult commitment to the church. So the wild oats that appear troublesome at first may eventually yield a fruitful harvest as adult members embrace the ways of Amish faith.

Family registers often hang on the walls of Amish homes. Quilts are prized for their quality and artistic designs.

The farmhouse studio of a
self-trained Amish artist.
Her sketches of Amish life
are in national demand.

Art

Amish culture has historically eschewed artistic expression. Several strands of their religious heritage have helped to stifle the artistic spirit. Descendants of the Anabaptist movement often disdained the images and art of "high" churches. Germinating over the years, these sentiments sometimes viewed works of art as vain idolatry—equivalents of the biblically forbidden graven images.

Moreover, the individualistic streak in artistic expression collides with the communal values of Amish culture. Art that exalts the individual is unwelcome. Hung or displayed, personal portraits call attention to the individual and the artist. Such expression, in the Amish mind, breeds pride and arrogance. Historically, homemade Amish dolls were typically faceless to avoid the appearance of a graven image and erase individual expression.

Amish culture is also rooted in the soil of practical rural values. Art—to be blunt—is an impractical, unnecessary frivolity. To rural peasants, eking out a living by the sweat of their brow, art was a waste of time. Pragmatic and useful activities are treasured in Amish culture, not the fantasies of individual artists. Abstract art with its multitude of interpretations intrigues the modern mind. The Amish, however, want to know if something works—is it practical and useful? Congealing together, these cultural sentiments almost sealed the fate of Amish art.

But the destiny of Amish art was not completely doomed. Expressions of folk art have bubbled out of Amish life over the centuries. Barbara Ebersole (1864–1922) was widely known for her fraktur—lovely artistic lettering. A dwarf, she designed colorful bookplates for Bibles and other family records. Her designs, which feature fancy hearts, tulips, and assorted flowers, top $3,000 at public auctions. Embroidered family registers, calendars, and genealogical charts have long decorated Amish walls. Quilt designs, garden flowers, and homemade crafts are age-old forms of artistic expression.

In recent years, the usefulness of Amish art has grown. Craft sales are soaring. Art has suddenly become a practical means of making a living in the face of diminishing farmland and rising tourism. A wide spectrum of artistic expression has blossomed in crafts of all sorts, but, all things considered, it remains folk art. Saws, shingles, metal disks, and other practical items are hand painted for sale. Needlework, cornhusk dolls, and quilts galore are a few of hundreds of items produced and sold by the Amish.

One artist complained that "it's okay to paint milk cans but not to display your work at art shows." But even that is changing. Some self-trained Amish artists are beginning to paint on canvas as well as to display and sell their work. One Amish artist was featured in *USA TODAY* in 1991. A first-time exhibit of Amish art appeared in the Lancaster region in 1991. Church leaders have permitted such ventures, especially for members with financial needs and when the art clearly involves "making a living" rather than displaying vainglory. But the new art remains entrapped in cultural shackles. The pastoral scenes on canvas are limited to depictions of actual Amish settings. Individuals are rarely drawn. And when they are, faces are never shown. Appearing on canvas and designed to be hung and enjoyed, the new Amish art remains practical, still hemmed in by cultural values—surely not abstractions of postmodern imaginations.

~·~ What is a Mother ~·~

It takes a Mother's LOVE to make a house a home, a place to be remembered, no matter where we roam... It takes a Mother's PATIENCE to bring a child up right, And her COURAGE and her CHEERFULNESS to make a dark day bright... It takes a Mother's THOUGHTFULNESS to mend the heart's deep "hurts", And her SKILL and her ENDURANCE to mend little socks and shirts... It takes a Mother's KINDNESS to forgive us when we err, To sympathize in trouble and bow her head in prayer... It takes a Mother's WISDOM to recognize our needs And to give us reassurance by her loving words and deeds. It takes a Mother's ENDLESS FAITH, her CONFIDENCE and TRUST To guide us through the pitfalls of selfishness and lust... And that is why in all this world there could not be another Who could fulfill God's purpose as completely as a Mother!

Motherhood is highly
esteemed in Amish life.

112

Women play a vital role in farming operations. This woman drives five horses pulling a hay baler.

A water wheel provides
power to pump water from
a well into a storage tank.
Diesel engines are
replacing water wheels and
windmills on many farms.

A storage tank (*left*) holds water for this farmstead. Water flows to the buildings by gravity. A white plastic bag in the foreground provides storage for corn silage.

BEAN

BROCCOLI

ZUCCHINI

OPE

PICKLES
1 Qt.
2.90

CHOW-CHOW
1 pt.
1.75

CHOW-CHOW
1 Qt.
3.00

CHOW-CHOW
1½ pt.
2.25

STRAWBERRY
JELLY
2.00

RHUBARB
JELLY
2.00

GRAPE

PEACH

1.25

.80

1.25

An Old Order Mennonite
buys produce from an
Amish girl at a roadside
stand. Hundreds of these
stands sell produce, quilts,
and handicrafts to tourists.

A young mother
heads homeward from a
shopping trip.

Sizing Up Tourism

European forebears of the Amish were violently persecuted for daring to be different. Today the Amish defiance of modern culture brings admiration and respect—enough to underwrite a massive tourist industry. The world, which the Amish have tried so hard to keep at bay, is now reaching out to them.

An Amish farmer dates the rise of Lancaster County tourism with the two hundredth birthday of the village of Intercourse in 1954. "Mix together the word *intercourse* and some Amish buggies," he said, "and you're bound to attract some tourists." An estimated five million tourists visit Lancaster County annually—some 300 visitors for each Amish person. Tourists spend over $400 million—about $25,000 per Amish person. Although visitors come to Lancaster County for many reasons, the Amish are certainly a major magnet.

Tourism is often a nuisance to the Amish and sometimes a source of humor. Cars and buses clog country roads. Clicking cameras, gawking strangers, and incessant questions soon become tiresome. One Amishwoman said, "We are opposed to having our souls marketed by having our sacred beliefs and traditions stolen from us and then distributed to tourists and sometimes having them mocked." In the words of an Amish minister, "The tourist attractions have converted our Amish land into a leisure lust playground." Tourism, in the Amish mind, symbolizes worldly pleasure. Deriding Amish values, tourists kill time, seek entertainment, and waste money.

Although tourism bothers the Amish soul, it also brings benefits. In recent years, hundreds of roadside stands have sprung up across the settlement, selling, among other things, quilts, crafts, vegetables, and baked goods. The roadside stands provide a convenient middle ground for tourist/Amish interactions. The roadside encounters allow tourists a fleeting glimpse of Amish life and bring welcome revenues to Amish households. The terms and times of discourse, however, are carefully regulated at a safe distance from Amish homes. An interesting compromise of sorts, these roadside stands offer visitors a taste of Amish life while boosting Amish profits.

Tourism brings more than economic benefits. In subtle ways, it bolsters collective self-esteem. An Amish statesman observed that with the rise of tourism, "We are no longer looked down upon." Said another, "We get loads of praise for our way of life." Although reluctant to admit pride, the Amish enjoy a quiet satisfaction in knowing their culture is worthy of such interest and respect. Tourism also creates expectations for Amish behavior. To discard the horse and buggy would not only break Amish tradition but also shatter expectations placed on the community by outside visitors.

Perhaps most importantly, tourism fortifies Amish bargaining power. Serving as the cultural magnet for tourism has strengthened the political muscle of the Amish when they negotiate with public officials over schools, highways, and zoning regulations. And occasionally elders make vague references to their biggest bargaining chip—migration. Thus, in an ironic twist of history, these despised European heretics have become not only esteemed objects of curiosity but brokers of political power as well.

Old-fashioned milk cans are used to transport water.

Witness

The feature film *Witness* placed images of the Amish on screens around the world. Lancaster Amish were surprised to learn that Paramount Pictures planned to shoot an Amish movie in their backyard. The filming of *Witness* in the summer of 1984 stirred controversy within the church.

The Amish have long objected to photographs of persons. Personal portraits call attention to the individual and cultivate the sins of pride and vanity. By elevating individuals above the community, portraits—in the Amish mind—exemplify the "graven images" condemned by Scripture. Moreover, the Amish eschew Hollywood movies as "dens of iniquity" that spew the vulgarities of sex and violence around the world. And clinging to the virtues of modesty and humility, the Amish have long deplored publicity and promotion.

With such values entrenched in their culture, the possibility of a Hollywood feature was abhorrent to Amish sensibilities. Beyond the cultural insult, some members suspected commercial motives. "We feel," said an Amishwoman, "that we are serving as a tool to lure tourists to Lancaster County." Indeed, the Pennsylvania Bureau of Motion Picture and TV Development, eager for national publicity and tourist revenues, had solicited Paramount to do a film on the Amish.

As the Paramount cameras began rolling in Lancaster County, Amish bishops forbade members to assist the production crews. "We can't stop them," said one Amishman, "but we don't have to help them. We don't want it. It doesn't belong here." Despite the resistance, Paramount solicited Amish help for staging and props. Church leaders made it clear that anyone aiding the project would be excommunicated. The breach of mis-

trust widened with the discovery that actress Kelly McGillis had lived in disguise for several days in an Amish home.

Members of the Amish community watched from afar as Harrison Ford, dressed in traditional garb, defended Amish ways with clenched fists in the village of Intercourse. The use of force by someone in Amish garb, even if he portrayed a sympathetic outsider, rankled Amish nerves. The filming prompted church leaders to protest to Pennsylvania's lieutenant governor as well as to other state and local officials. Said one Amishman, "If our principles were to fight, I feel we could go to court and get an injunction on the basis of misrepresenting the Amish, but this is not our way."

By the time the shooting was finished, an agreement was struck between Amish elders and state officials. The settlement stipulated, among other things, that the state would not promote the Amish as subjects for feature films or television productions. But the face-saving agreement contained no promises to blockade a future *Witness*.

The violence of a cop thriller framed by pastoral scenes of Amish countryside created a dramatic clash of images. Despite an implausible plot and many cultural errors, *Witness* did introduce many people around the world to Amish ways.

Gathering wildflowers
after school.

Cutting weeds along a fencerow. The elderly in Amish society do not receive Social Security or Medicare.

Government Ties

Do the Amish pay their fair share of taxes or merely feed at public coffers? In company with other Americans, they do pay tribute to Caesar—federal and state income taxes, sales taxes, and real estate and personal property taxes. Indeed, they pay school taxes twice—for both public and Amish schools. Scant use of motor vehicles results, of course, in fewer gasoline taxes. Following biblical injunctions, the Amish pay all levied taxes except Social Security, from which they are exempt.

The Amish view Social Security as a national insurance program, not a tax. Congressional legislation passed in 1965 exempts self-employed persons who object to Social Security for religious reasons. Amish persons employed in Amish businesses are also exempted by congressional legislation. Those who don't qualify for the exemption—Amish employees in non-Amish businesses—must pay Social Security without reaping its benefits. Paying Social Security without collecting benefits feels, in the words of one Amishman, "like buying a dead horse." Thus, most church members neither pay into nor tap Social Security. Bypassing Social Security not only severs the Amish from old age payments, it also closes the spigot of Medicare and Medicaid.

The Amish object to government aid for several reasons. The church, they contend, should assume responsibility for the social welfare of its own members. The aged, infirm, senile, disabled, and retarded are cared for, whenever possible, within extended family networks. To turn the care of these folks over to the state would abdicate a fundamental tenet of faith—the care of one's brothers and sisters in the church.

Furthermore, federal aid in the form of Social Security or Medicare would surely erode dependency on the church and undercut its programs of mutual aid. The Amish have organized several programs of mutual aid to assist members with fire and storm damages as well as with medical expenses. During severe summer droughts, disaster relief funds or farm products are shared with needy Amish beyond the Lancaster settlement.

Government subsidies, or what the Amish call "handouts," are strongly opposed. Championing self-sufficiency and the separation of church and state, the Amish worry that the hand that feeds them will also control them. Over the years they have stubbornly refused direct subsidies, even for agricultural programs designed for farmers in distress. Federal cow buyout programs to limit milk production and payments to keep farmland idle have all been shunned—sometimes to the amazement of government bureaucrats. Amish farmers do, however, receive indirect subsidies through agricultural price-support programs.

The Amish have a long history of caring for their own and thus have little need for public welfare. They can hardly be called freeloaders or social parasites. On the whole, they tap few public funds. Indeed, by paying their fair share of taxes and siphoning off few public dollars, they not only take care of their own but also make significant contributions to the public good.

123

Barley, corn, and wheat are grain crops cultivated by the Amish. This field of bearded barley will be harvested in late June.

Wheat growing is on the decline. This binder is an offspring of Cyrus McCormick's famous reaper.

After drying in shocks,
wheat is threshed with a
steam engine the old-
fashioned way.

A modern baler attached to the thresher packs wheat straw in bales for storage. The grain is loaded on a truck.

Every Amish barn has a
mouser.

Wishing wells manu-
factured in this Amish
shop are sold in large
numbers in the eastern
United States. A
non-Amish distributor
prepares to deliver a
gazebo and some yard
toys.

Social Gatekeepers

Although Lancaster's Amish maintain lines of separation from the world, they are also entangled with it. Farm and business profits fluctuate with the rise and fall of prices in the broader economic market. Beyond financial ties, the Amish are linked to the outside world through three types of social gatekeepers—intermediaries who regulate the flow of information between the two worlds. Direct access to public information is somewhat limited, since the Amish are insulated from mass media and public education. Thus, the need for intermediaries who funnel ideas into the Amish community from the outside world.

Amish entrepreneurs are insiders who open the gates to Amish society. Even though their eighth-grade education would seem to put them at a disadvantage, they interact well with outsiders. Fluent in English, well-traveled, and sometimes well-read, they live in both worlds. Comfortable with non-Amish peers, these self-trained managers straddle the cultural fence separating the Amish from the modern world. As inside gatekeepers they use information from external contacts to bolster their own work as well as the efforts of the community. Although some take correspondence courses or attend short-term technical schools, the bulk of information is gleaned from informal conversation with clients, sales agents, suppliers, and a variety of professionals.

The Amish community has no professionals of its own, since youth do not attend high school or college. Church members do, however, use the services of professionals in the larger community—midwives, doctors, dentists, optometrists, accountants, lawyers, veterinarians, bankers, and farm consultants. These

131

Many Amish men work on construction crews.

external gatekeepers provide not only technical services but also general information and counsel. Salespeople who visit Amish farms and businesses channel news into the community. Interactions with these professionals as well as with non-Amish friends and neighbors weave the Amish into the larger cultural fabric.

A third class of gatekeepers are non-Amish who advocate the virtues of Amish life. An assortment of friends, neighbors, and professionals encircle Amish society like a friendly cocoon. Largely unorganized, these friends share a common interest in preserving Amish culture for a variety of reasons. Since the Amish often hesitate to defend their rights, speak out in public, or flex their political muscle, these protectors of Amish ways spring to life around specific issues—land

preservation, highway construction, zoning, tourism, and other threats to Amish life. These friends, trained in the politics of power, speak on behalf of the Amish— sometimes quietly in backstage corridors and other times loudly in public meetings.

Such brokers of power arrange discussions between Amish leaders and political officials, pull the levers of bureaucracy on behalf of their Amish friends, and, when necessary, seek legal solutions that favor them. These gatekeepers sometimes marshal large numbers of Amish to public meetings. Orchestrated by non-Amish friends, the presence of hundreds of Amish at a public hearing was one factor that derailed plans for a major highway that would have sliced through the heart of Amish farmland. Thus, the various gatekeepers provide essential conduits of information and influence for a society that limits formal education and shuns mass media.

Amish neighbors chat
outside Zimmerman's
Store in the village of
Intercourse.

Dried ear corn is harvested in the fall. A wagon with rubber tires is permitted because it was rented from a non-Amish neighbor.

A gasoline engine powers
this elevator, which fills a
corn bin.

Dried ear corn awaits use
in winter.

Zoning and sewer regulations required moving this stone Amish farmhouse. A non-Amish contractor was hired to move the house across the road to the upper left.

Zoning Regulations

Shrinking farmland and a spiraling Amish population created a host of new problems for Lancaster's Amish in the 1980s. Urbanization catapulted them into a maze of regulations heretofore unknown. In bygone years, they simply added retirement apartments to their homes as necessary. Farmers had never worried about polluting streams with manure runoff, but in the late eighties and early nineties the Amish were sparring with a host of new regulations.

In the winter of 1989, the church was jolted when two Amish farmers were fined for permitting barnyard water to spill into nearby streams. With some 25 percent of Pennsylvania's livestock in Lancaster County, manure and fertilizer runoff had become a chief culprit in the Chesapeake Bay's pollution. Declining farm size, high-density farming, growing concentrations of animals, and greater use of chemical fertilizer exacerbated the problem. Some Amish farmers bristled at the growing regulations, but others cooperated with local officials and sought to control farm pollution. Indeed, several Amish farmers visited the Chesapeake Bay region to learn about the problem firsthand. Upon their return, they developed experimental machines to dehydrate manure in order to reduce pollution.

Another flashpoint in zoning regulations involved the construction of new buildings. Squeezed off the land, many farmers began cottage industries on their farms—sometimes retrofitting old buildings, but other times constructing new ones. Farming areas, zoned for agriculture, had restrictions on commercial and retail use. In dozens of cases in the 1980s and early 1990s, Amish entrepreneurs clashed with zoning officials over exceptions, exemptions, and acceptable uses of land.

Differing regulations in each township complicated the problem.

In many instances, the Amish worked in tandem with local officials toward amiable settlements. However, townships sometimes prosecuted those who deliberately overstepped zoning ordinances. Some townships developed special regulations for farm-based Amish businesses. And in the early nineties, the Lancaster County Planning Commission offered townships model guidelines for farm-based businesses. These and other attempts aimed to address the special needs of the Amish community.

Residential zoning also stirred Amish ire. Some townships forbade the construction of retirement apartments, typically annexed to Amish homes. Farmers were sometimes denied permits to build a second house on their property for their offspring; or, if permitted, they had to pay $10,000 or more for a variety of water and sewer tests before beginning construction. Public officials worried that zoning enforcement would spur Amish migrations.

County leaders made special efforts to consult with Amish elders. As zoning irritations peaked in the fall of 1989, Pennsylvania's governor, Robert Casey, made a quiet, unpublicized trip to an Amish home to listen to Amish leaders. Within a few months, state legislators invited members of the Amish community, zoning officers, and officials of the Pennsylvania Department of Environmental Resources to several public meetings where state officials played down the bite of regulations and urged zoning officers to "use more common sense."

Scooters—a compromise
between walking and
driving—are used by many
Amish children. This
young girl rides in the
village of Intercourse.

Thoroughbred trotting
horses, retired from
the racetracks are often
purchased to pull
carriages.

Neighbors chat along a
country road. Horseshoes
and narrow steel wheels
often make ruts in
macadam roadways.

The Motor Vehicle Maze

Automobile use perplexes outsiders. Members of Lancaster's Amish settlement are permitted to ride in motor vehicles but not to own or drive them. This apparent, even hypocritical, double standard begins to make sense within the corridors of Amish history.

Automobiles gained popularity in the second decade of the twentieth century. They freed persons to travel independently, whenever and wherever they pleased. The auto, a symbol of American individualism and independence, liberated people from train and trolley schedules, broke the confines of geography, and splintered the provincialism of rural life.

But for a rural people who strove to remain separate from the world, the very name of this new invention spelled trouble. *Auto*matic *mobil*ity was a menace to a community that hoped to stay together. Automatic things signaled a loss of control, and mobility had little lure for folks who hoped to avoid city life. Given the keys to a car, individuals might drive away—far away to urban worlds of vice and pleasure. Church members driving about in cars would be out of control, free-floating, and independent. Individuals might also use cars to flaunt their status, power, and wealth—disrupting the equality of Amish life. And cars would surely accelerate the pace of things.

The car collided with the very core of Amish culture. It symbolized the delights of modernity—freedom, acceleration, power, mobility, autonomy, and individualism. Automobiles enticed an individuated, mobile society—but not a stable, local group who cherished community integration and separation from the world. If church members were permitted to drive about in cars, their ties to local church districts would unravel. The car, in short, threatened to pull the community apart.

Sensing the danger, church leaders placed a taboo on car *ownership* about 1915. *Use* of motor vehicles, however, varied by church district in the first half of the century as members sometimes rode with non-Amish neighbors. By midcentury, the use of motor vehicles for business, emergencies, and social visits was on the rise. As the Amish settlement expanded, it became difficult to travel to outlying areas by horse and carriage in a single day. Amish cottage industries, flourishing in the 1970s and 1980s, accelerated the use of motor vehicles. Businesses today hire vehicles to transport supplies and deliver products. Mobile carpentry crews travel to construction sites by hired van and truck. Some businesses have a non-Amish employee who provides a vehicle for company use.

Non-Amish neighbors began offering "taxi" service on a regular basis in the fifties. Dozens of non-Amish drivers now earn full or supplemental income by providing taxi service within the settlement as well as to distant sites. Families, friends, and neighbors often travel together in hired vans to social gatherings, sometimes out of state.

The firm line between the use and ownership of motor vehicles illustrates another negotiated compromise between modernity and tradition. A practical solution, it keeps the car at bay and controls its negative side effects, all the while using it to enhance community ties and bolster business. Restricted mobility keeps families together, holds work near home, and reinforces social interaction within church districts. Controlled use of the car keeps faith with Amish tradition while also giving some freedom to maneuver in the larger society.

Out-of-state Amish visit
Meyers Cemetery in
Lancaster County. Vans
and buses are often
chartered for special trips.

Returning home from
market.

Carriage wheels are
manufactured in Amish
shops.

Carriage bodies are manufactured from fiberglass in this Amish shop.

The complete carriage is assembled at another shop. Traditional in style and color, Amish carriages have hydraulic brakes, permapane windshields, and battery-powered wipers, turn signals, lights, and flashers.

A variety of upholstery
styles and accessories are
available in new carriages.

Selective Use of Technology

Popular images construe the Amish as organic farmers who milk their cows by hand, but Lancaster's Old Order Amish spoil this caricature of Amish life. They do prefer the ways of nature, but they certainly do not shun modern technology. A wide array of technology aids work and comfort in kitchens, barns, and shops. Technology is selectively used and sometimes harnessed in special ways.

Homemakers typically use, among dozens of other common household items, spray starch, detergents, instant pudding, disposable diapers, and permanent press fabrics. Modern bathrooms, the latest gas appliances, and some pneumatic equipment are common in Amish households. Except for a few battery-powered gadgets, electrical appliances and lights are missing from Amish homes. Washing machines are often powered by gasoline engines or air pressure. Electric dryers and air conditioners, of course, are not found. Water is heated by gas hot-water heaters. Homes are normally warmed by kerosene or coal heaters.

A wide array of technology supports farming operations—automatic milkers, tractors, elevators, welders, and electric cow trainers powered by batteries. Pesticides, insecticides, preservatives, and chemical fertilizers are widely used, as are modern veterinary practices. Although frowned upon historically, artificial insemination of dairy cattle is becoming widespread. But there are limits here as well. Embryo transplants are taboo. Silo unloaders, milk pipelines, milking parlors, automatic barn cleaners, and self-propelled equipment have not received the blessing of the church.

Shops and cottage industries employ a vast array of mechanical equipment, albeit hydraulic and pneumatic-powered. Some craftsmen work with plastic and fiberglass materials. Small 12-volt motors, electrical inverters, and diesel engines energize shop equipment. Electronic cash registers, digital scales, and electric calculators powered by inverters are commonplace. Businessmen sometimes use credit cards. But again, some limits lace this world. Computers and standard electrical equipment—with some special exceptions—are forbidden. Carpentry crews may use standard electrical tools at construction sites, but not at home.

The lines of discretion that restrict the use of technology are drawn from many sources. Some of the limits flow from fears that large farms and shops will disrupt the order and equality of community life. Other restrictions are designed to stymie the cultural contamination that might come via computers and televisions. Still other guidelines rest on historic taboos—holding firm over the years—that preserve Amish identity.

Technology is also bridled when its long-term consequences appear to threaten the welfare of the community. An elderly bishop said, "If I had a car it might not hurt any, but for the oncoming generation, you ought to be willing to sacrifice for them." New forms of technology are not moralized as sinful or evil; rather, they are tagged as "worldly," "unwise," "too handy," or simply as "unnecessary," meaning they are a menace to the spiritual and social welfare of the community.

151

Lapp's Carriage Shop
restored this
historic carriage for
David Rockefeller.

Civic Participation

Religious commitments to remain separate from the world govern Amish interaction in the larger society. Unbridled participation not only would violate the tenets of separation but also might eventually dissolve the boundaries of Amish identity. Although the Amish live outside the social mainstream, they are, nevertheless, good neighbors. Friendships flourish with neighbors and sometimes even with tourists. Amish persons interact freely with outsiders via occupational roles—in retail sales, at farmers' markets, and as cooks and waitresses in restaurants. Others develop long term friendships working as domestic aids in private homes. The ties are pleasant, but they do not flower into the intimacies of romance or business partnerships. Such relationships, to use biblical language, are considered "unequal yoking" with unbelievers.

Amish participation in outside organizations is selective, informal, and locally oriented. Members typically do not join service clubs (Rotary, Kiwanis, Lions), country clubs, swimming pool associations, Boy Scouts or Girl Scouts of America, Little League teams, or community organizations such as the Red Cross. Membership in professional and business organizations is also generally taboo. Although some church districts discourage membership, many farmers have joined the Dairy Herd Improvement Association. Those who do are careful not to have their participation or their achievements publicized. In some communities, Amishmen actively participate in volunteer fire companies. Several fire companies sponsor benefit auctions—strongly supported by the Amish—with annual sales topping several hundred thousand dollars.

Amish members readily assist non-Amish neighbors in times of disaster, fire, and illness. Carpentry crews frequently travel out of state by bus or van under the auspices of Mennonite Disaster Service to rebuild homes destroyed by flood, hurricane, or tornado. Lancaster's Amish, for example, made many trips to aid the victims of Hurricane Hugo in South Carolina. Church members also support benefit auctions, garage sales, and historical celebrations in the larger community.

Attendance at public events and places such as fairs, carnivals, dances, amusement parks, and theaters is forbidden for church members. Prior to baptism, however, some youth may sneak a peek at such events or even join community softball teams or racquetball clubs. Selective participation in civic affairs honors the age-old principle of separation from the world, reinforces the lines of Amish identity, and funnels social interaction within ethnic networks.

153

Corn fodder is baled in
the fall for bedding.

Stacking bales of fodder.

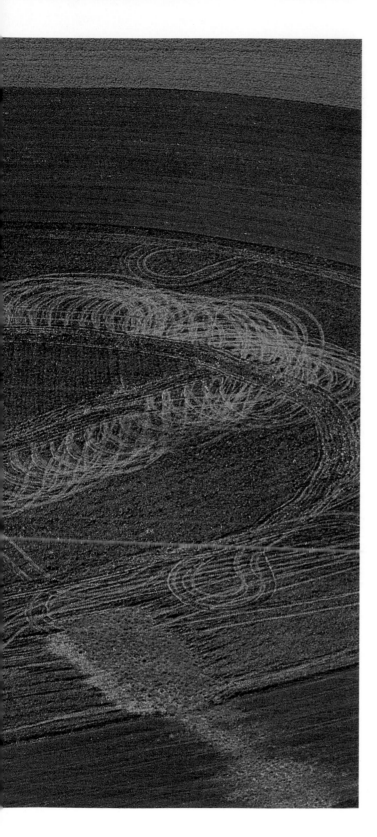

Family graveyards are
often surrounded by
farmland.

Dying Gracefully

A funeral director observed that the Amish accept
death in graceful ways. With the elderly living at home,
the gradual loss of health prepares family members for
the final passage. And in times of suffering, death
comes as a blessing. Accompanied by quiet grief, death
comes as the final benediction to a good life and entry
into the bliss of eternity. Funeral preparations reflect
core Amish values—simplicity, humility, and mutual
aid—as family and friends yield to eternal verities.

The community springs into action at word of a
death. Family and friends in the local church district
assume barn and household chores, freeing the immediate family. Well-established funeral rituals unburden
the family from worrisome choices. Three couples are
appointed to extend invitations and supervise funeral
arrangements—food preparation, seating arrangements, and the coordination of a large number of
horses and carriages.

In the Lancaster settlement, a non-Amish undertaker moves the body to a funeral home for embalming.
The body—without cosmetic improvements—returns
to the home in a simple, hardwood coffin within a day.
Family members of the same sex dress the body in
white. White garments symbolize the final passage into
a new and better existence, eternal life. Women often
are garbed in the white cape and apron worn at their
wedding. Tailoring the white clothes prior to death
helps to prepare the family for the season of grief.

Friends and relatives visit the family and view the
body in a room on the first floor of the home for two
days prior to the funeral. Meanwhile, community
members dig the grave by hand in a nearby family
cemetery as others oversee the daily chores of the be-

157

reaved. Several hundred guests attend the funeral in a barn or home, typically on the morning of the third day after death. During the simple hour-and-a-half-long service, ministers read hymns and Scripture, offer prayers, and preach a sermon. Singing and eulogies are missing, and there are no flowers, burial gowns, burial tents, limousines, or sculpted monuments.

The hearse, a large black carriage pulled by horses, leads a long procession of other carriages to the burial ground on the edge of a farm. A brief viewing and graveside service mark the return of dust to dust. Pall-bearers lower the coffin and shovel soil into the grave as the bishop reads a hymn. Small, equal-sized tombstones mark the place of the deceased in the commu-

nity of equality. Close friends and family members then return to the home for a meal prepared by members of the local congregation.

Bereaved women, especially close relatives, may signal their mourning by wearing a black dress in public settings for as long as a year. A painful separation laced with grief, death is nevertheless received in the spirit of Gelassenheit—the ultimate surrender to God's higher ways. Surrounded by family and friends and comforted by predictable ritual filled with religious meanings, the separation is humane by modern standards. The tears flow, but the sobs are restrained as people submit quietly to the rhythms of divine purpose. From cradle to grave, the mysteries of life and death unravel in the context of loving families and supportive ritual.

Equal-size tombstones symbolize equality among adults in Amish life. Small stones mark the graves of children.

A mule takes a midday break before returning to the fields.

The long horizontal
building houses poultry on
this dairy farm.

A courting couple heads
toward a Sunday evening
singing.

Courting on a chilly day.

165

Carriages gathered for a
wedding.

Weddings

The wedding season is a festive time in Amish life. On the heels of the harvest, the Lancaster community hosts some 150 weddings on Tuesdays and Thursdays from late October through early December. Fifteen weddings may be scattered across the settlement on the same day. Typically staged in the home of the bride, these joyous events involve upwards of 350 guests, two meals, singing, snacks, festivities, and a three-hour service.

Young persons typically marry in their early twenties. Bishops will only perform marriages for members of the church. Young men begin growing a beard—the functional equivalent of a wedding ring—soon after their marriage. They are expected to have a "full stand" by the springtime communion. The church does not arrange marriages, but it does place its blessing on the pair through an old ritual. Prior to the wedding, the groom takes a letter signed by church elders to the bride's deacon testifying to the groom's "good standing" in his home district. The bride's deacon then meets with her to verify the marriage plans.

The wedding day is an enormous undertaking for the bride's family as well as for relatives and friends who assist with preparations. Efforts to clean up the property, paint rooms, fix furniture, pull weeds, and pave driveways, among other things, begin weeks in advance. The logistics of preparing two meals as well as snacks for several hundred guests are taxing. The day before the wedding the groom, according to custom, decapitates several dozen chickens. The noontime wedding menu includes "chicken roast"—small pieces of chicken mixed with bread filling—mashed potatoes, gravy, creamed celery, pepper cabbage, and other items. Desserts include pears, peaches, and puddings and, of course, dozens of pies and hundreds of cookies and doughnuts.

The three-hour service—without flowers, rings, solos, or instrumental music—is similar to an Amish worship service. The wedding includes congregational singing, prayers, and wedding vows, as well as two sermons. Four single friends serve the bride and groom as attendants; however, no one is designated maid of honor or best man. Amish brides typically make their own wedding dresses from blue or purple material crafted in traditional styles. In addition to the groom's new but customary black coat and vest, he and his attendants often wear small black bow ties.

Games, snacks, and singing follow the noon meal, which involves several seatings. Young people are paired off somewhat randomly for the singing. Following the evening meal, another more lively singing takes place in which couples who are dating pair off—arousing considerable interest because this may be their first public appearance. Festivities may continue until nearly midnight as guests gradually leave. Some guests, invited to several weddings on the same day, may rotate between them.

Newly married couples usually set up housekeeping in the spring after their wedding. Until then, the groom may live at the bride's home or continue to live with his parents. In lieu of a traditional honeymoon, couples visit relatives on weekends during the winter months. Several newlywed couples may visit together, sometimes staying overnight at the home of close relatives. During this honeymoon of visitation, family and friends present gifts to the newlyweds, adding to the bride's dowry—which often consists of some furniture.

Amish weddings are
usually held on Tuesdays
and Thursdays in
November and December.
This one was attended by
over 400 guests.

The seasons regulate the
rhythms of Amish life.
Snow blankets an Amish
farmstead.

Products of playful
imaginations.

This Amish bakery
provides cookies, pastries,
and decorations for the
festivities of the Christmas
season.

Holidays

Seasons and holidays shape the Amish year. Sharing some national holidays with non-Amish neighbors and adding others of their own, the Amish have created a calendar that underscores both their participation in, and separation from, the larger world. As conscientious objectors, they have little enthusiasm for patriotic days with a military flair. Memorial Day, Veterans Day, and the Fourth of July are barely noticed. Even Labor Day stirs little interest. The witches and goblins of Halloween feel foreign to Amish spirits. Pumpkins may be displayed, but without cut faces. Halloween parties are never held. And Martin Luther King, Jr.? His birthday slips by unnoticed in the rural enclaves of Lancaster County. For the most part, these national outings fall outside the Amish calendar.

Amish holidays follow the rhythm of the seasons and traditional religious celebrations. These furloughs from work imbue the Amish year with a religious tone. A day for prayer and fasting precedes the October communion service. The flurry of fall weddings provides ample holidays of another sort. Those without wedding invitations celebrate Thanksgiving Day with turkey dinners and family gatherings. New Year's Day is a quiet time for family gatherings, not intoxicating parties and marathon football games that reflect the ways of a foreign culture. A second day is added to the celebrations of Christmas, Easter, and Pentecost. The regular holiday, a sacred time, flows with quiet family activities. The following day—second Christmas, Easter Monday, and Pentecost Monday—provides time for recreation, visiting, and sometimes shopping. Ascension Day, prior to Pentecost, is a holiday for visiting, fishing, and other forms of recreation. "More visiting takes place on these springtime holidays," said one Amishman, "than at any other time."

Christmas and Easter festivities are spared from commercial trappings. Families exchange Christmas cards and gifts. Some presents are homemade crafts and practical gifts, but increasingly many are store bought. Homes are decorated with greens, but Christmas trees, stockings, special lights, Santa Claus, and mistletoe are missing. Although eggs are sometimes painted and children may be given a basket of candy, Easter bunnies rarely, if ever, visit Amish homes. These sacred holidays revolve around religious customs, family gatherings, and quiet festivities rather than commercial trinkets and worldly hubbub.

Birthdays are celebrated at home and school in quiet but pleasant ways, with cakes and gifts—but not in large-scale parties filled with clowns, balloons, and noisemakers. Parents often provide a special snack of cookies or popsicles for their child to share with school friends to honor a birthday. Holiday festivities in the Amish world reaffirm religious roots, strengthen family ties, and underscore the lines of separation from the larger culture.

A young boy on his way on
an icy day.

A game of hockey on a
winter afternoon.

The Future of Amish Society

What of the fate of Amish society? Will the Amish of the twenty-first century still ride in buggies and shun electricity? Might Lancaster's Amish migrate en masse to rural hideaways of other states or even other countries? Will urbanization devour Amish life beyond recognition? Some scholars in the mid-1950s predicted the demise of Amish society. They were obviously wrong. Indeed, the Amish have flourished in the most modern, most industrialized century of all times.

The future shape of Amish life escapes prediction. Particular outcomes will be shaped not only by unforeseen external forces—market prices, government regulations, rates of urbanization—but also by internal politics and the sentiments of particular Amish leaders. A variety of unpredictable variables will determine the destiny of the Amish journey. Without a centralized decision-making process—let alone a strategic planning council—new directions are unpredictable. Migrations in the past have taken the form of grassroots initiatives spurred by the interests of scattered families or a particular church district. Crystal ball scenarios are tenuous, at best, but past behavior may offer some clues to the future.

Three habits of the past will likely shape Amish responses to the future: high-density farming, alternative work, and emigration. Despite soaring land prices and encroaching urbanization, a portion of Lancaster's Amish will probably continue to till the soil of their ancestors into the twenty-first century. One businessman said, "The Amish in Lancaster feel that Lancaster's our home—we don't move as quickly as the Amish in other states." Farmland preservation, which the Amish are now beginning to support, as well as emotional ties to the ancestral soil and cemeteries of their oldest North American settlement, are likely to tether some to the land. But farming practices will change. One Amishman raises hydroponic tomatoes, which float on fertilized water in greenhouses. Other families are raising produce on a few acres of land. More high-density ventures of this sort will probably emerge in the future.

The willingness of many Amish to leave their plows for cottage industries in the 1970s and 1980s signaled a dramatic change of direction in the three hundred-year Amish voyage. As cottage industries blossom and bring change to Amish life, they will increase interaction with the outside world. Generating substantial income, these business endeavors will surely alter the class structure and cultural face of Amish society over the years.

But the love of farming lies deep in the Amish heart. Some families will likely migrate out of state in search of fertile soil. Throughout their history the Amish have readily moved in the face of persecution and adversity. Indeed, they have been leaving Lancaster County for many years. A settlement was planted in the state of Maryland in 1940. In the 1960s and 1970s, ten new settlements with some three thousand members were established in other Pennsylvania counties.

Some Amish have begun moving farther away. In 1989 and 1991, Lancaster families organized new settlements in Kentucky and Indiana. Trekking 650 miles west to Parke County, Indiana, farmers bought tillable land for $1,000 an acre—six to eight times below Lancaster prices. A sudden, massive migration, however, is unlikely. But steady dribbles of Lancaster emigrants to other rural areas of the United States will surely continue.

The cultural flavor of twenty-first-century Amish life eludes forecast, but one emergent pattern is clear. Settlements pressed by urbanization are the most progressive in outlook and the most updated in technology. In short, they are the most willing to negotiate with modernity. Rural homesteads beyond the tentacles of urban sprawl remain the best place to preserve traditional Amish ways. If the Amish can educate and retain their children, make a living without merchandizing their souls, and restrain interaction with the larger world, they will probably flourish into the twenty-first century. But one thing is certain: diversity between settlements will surely grow, mocking the staid stereotypes of Amish life.

Amish society stands in stark contrast to the modern world.

Struggles of the Modern Soul

Why do the Amish intrigue us? They are, of course, different, but mere difference is not enough. Is it their stubborn courage in thwarting the tide of progress that stirs our curiosity? Perhaps we are fascinated by their sense of place, their strength of identity, their apparent security, and even their sense of confidence. We admire their ability to fashion a humane system that ranks high on the scale of human satisfaction. These elusive qualities evoke yearnings in the modern soul. In the midst of a fragmented world, the Amish sense of wholeness lures and inspires us. Perhaps they intrigue us because they have discovered ways to fulfill the deeper longings of the human heart. But why are we charmed by folks who repudiate many of the esteemed values of modern life—individualism, tolerance, choice, and diversity?

Amish ways do fascinate us, but they also rankle modern sensitivities. Talk of humility flies in the face of our cherished individualism, which seeks self-fulfillment and personal achievement at every turn. We are troubled by people who limit education, restrict occupations, curb personal freedom, and stifle artistic expression. Their pleas for obedience—to yield to the community—appear oppressive, sexist, and suffocating by modern standards. The provincialism of Amish culture irritates our modern penchant for diversity and pluralism. A well-rounded, well-traveled cosmopolitanism is the charm of modern culture. The intolerance and rigidity of Amish life surely squelches the human spirit and cultivates a myopic world-view. Indeed, it squanders enormous human potential. Consider the hundreds of possible pilots, physicians, nurses, lawyers, and engineers who plow in Amish fields.

The conformity of Amish life also nags at us. Fidelity to tradition—conforming to church regulations, driving identical carriages, dressing alike—cultivates a bland, even boring uniformity. The Amish disdain for critical thinking and scientific exploration collides with modern views. Such habits nurture a herd mentality that hampers human dignity by promoting thoughtless ritualism. On the modern screen these folks appear as puppets of their culture, controlled by the strings of religious tradition. Surely it would be a dismal world if everyone joined the Amish and shunned science, higher education, open inquiry, computer technology, and global communication.

But the Amish also torment the modern soul. Indeed, their communal constraints have crafted a secure social home without the aid of higher education. The unemployed and uninsured are missing in Amish society. Widows and orphans, the destitute and disabled, are encompassed within the bonds of community. A spontaneous, humane social security springs into action in the face of fire, disability, sickness, senility, and death. Drug abuse, alcoholism, and poverty are rare. Youth are occasionally arrested for disturbing the peace or driving under the influence, but violent crime is nil. Divorce is unheard of, and the elderly age within a caring circle of family and friends. Amish suicide and mental illness rates dip below the norm. As in any society there are unhappy marriages, cantankerous personalities, and family feuds. But all things considered, the quality of Amish life appears remarkably robust by modern standards.

Youthful teachers master the craft of teaching without the benefit of college—let alone high school. And the eight-grade Amish schools produce entrepreneurs who are able to develop and manage thriving cottage industries. Unlike modern work—often fraught with alienation—Amish work has not been robbed of meaning, human dignity, or a delight in craftsmanship.

Amish mothers deliver and raise their babies without the aid of self-help books. Seminars on wellness, assertiveness training, stress management, and time management are unheard of here. Immediate and extended families provide a network of care throughout the life cycle.

Moreover, the Amish system functions almost effortlessly—without consultants, strategic plans, or long-term economic forecasts. The more wars that modern people declare on poverty, ignorance, and drug abuse, the more things appear to go awry. Somehow, with little effort, the Amish seem firmly in charge of things.

Most troubling of all to outsiders is the fear that, despite our smorgasbord of high-tech gadgets, abundant leisure, and heroic efforts to control things, the Amish might actually be more satisfied—even happier—than we are. That anxiety haunts and, indeed, it torments the modern soul—perhaps it's why we stop to ponder Amish ways. Are they merely a curious residual, a cultural relic of bygone days? Or do they offer a prototype of postmodern ways?

Amish ways trouble us because they unravel our assumptions about bigness, progress, diversity, education, freedom, individual dignity, and tradition. They propose that tolerance and individualism may have to yield when they spoil the virtues of an orderly community and secure personal identities. The upside-down values of Amish life esteem tradition as much as change, lift communal goals above personal ones, prefer work over consumption, and place personal sacrifice on a par with pleasure. They question if "newer," "bigger," and "faster" necessarily mean "better." Moreover, they contend that living cooperatively in orderly communities is the supreme value.

The wisdom afloat in this reservoir of tradition suggests that some things are best removed from individual choice, that firm limits and clear boundaries may best preserve human dignity over the generations. It is possible, the Amish argue, to tame technology, to control the size of things, to bridle bureaucracy, and to hold things to a human scale.

Make no mistake, these virtues come with a price—one that few outsiders are willing to pay. These communal outcomes require sacrifice—giving up assertive individualism. They require forgoing individual preference in dress, transportation, and education. They require accepting restrictions on convenience, friendship, marriage, mobility, and occupational choice. They require avoiding commercial leisure and shunning mass media. They pivot on a religious world-view. In short, such outcomes require the embrace of a different world—a world where the welfare of the community supersedes individual freedom, a world that by modern benchmarks is provincial and restrictive.

The costs of being Amish are high, but the benefits—identity, meaning, and belonging—are surely precious commodities in the midst of social fragmentation. The satisfactions bequeathed by traditional ways may compensate for the necessary sacrifices. First-time observers of Amish society are surprised by the latitude of personal freedom within the fences of Amish life—surprised by the dignity afforded individuals within the limits of constraint. Thus, in the larger scheme of things the discipline that appears to hamper the human spirit may, indeed, shape the marrow of a satisfied soul.

Suggested Readings

The classic treatment of the Amish of North America is John A. Hostetler's *Amish Society* (Baltimore: Johns Hopkins University Press), originally published in 1963 and now available in a fourth revised edition. Hostetler, who was born and reared in an Amish community, takes the reader inside Amish culture and explains the nature of Amish religious beliefs and ceremonies, community and family life, separatism, mutual-aid practices, tensions with worldly values, and interactions with outsiders. Long considered the definitive ethnography of Amish culture, *Amish Society* focuses on the larger Amish settlements. Also invaluable is John A. Hostetler's edited collection, *Amish Roots: A Treasury of History, Wisdom, and Lore* (Baltimore: Johns Hopkins University Press, 1989). This collection of more than 150 rare and unusual letters and journal entries, poems and stories, riddles, legends, and bits of family lore offers a unique view of Amish life from colonial times to the present. The Amish story is told by the Amish themselves, by their friends and neighbors, and by others who understand Amish ways.

In *Tradition and Transition* (Scottdale, Pa.: Herald Press, 1991), Paton Yoder describes social upheavals among the Amish in the last half of the nineteenth century as they coped with the early pressures of industrialization. A series of books written by Stephen Scott and published by Good Books deals with special topics of Amish life, such as weddings, transportation, dress, and alternative forms of energy. Scott's books provide a readable introduction to a variety of interesting issues surrounding North America's Amish.

Many of the themes discussed in this book, *Old Order Amish,* are developed in greater depth in Donald B. Kraybill's book *The Riddle of Amish Culture* (Baltimore: Johns Hopkins University Press, 1989). This social history of the Amish settlement in Lancaster County, Pennsylvania, describes how the Amish have flourished in the midst of modernity. To the outsider, the habits and customs of the Amish abound with contradictions. For example, why do they ride in cars but refuse to drive them? But the most intriguing puzzle of all is the secret of their survival in the twentieth century. How did the Amish of North America manage to grow from a meager band of 5,000 to over 130,000 today? *Riddle* quickly became a definitive study of social change in the Amish community. Kraybill also explores eighteen perplexing puzzles of Amish culture in *The Puzzles of Amish Life* (Intercourse, Pa.: Good Books, 1990).

The Amish and the State, a collection of original essays edited by Donald B. Kraybill (Baltimore: Johns Hopkins University Press, 1993), chronicles the many conflicts between the Amish and the state in the twentieth century on such matters as Social Security, education, health care, military service, slow-moving vehicles, zoning, and other First Amendment issues. The best overview of Amish conflicts with the state in the field of education is found in a series of essays edited by Albert N. Keim, entitled *Compulsory Education and the Amish* (Boston: Beacon Press, 1975). Also, John A. Hostetler and Gertrude E. Huntington offer insightful views of childhood socialization in *Amish Children* (New York: Harcourt Brace Jovanovich, 1992).

Index

187

Lucian Niemeyer was born in Essen, Germany, in 1937. He emigrated to the United States in 1939 on the last boat out of Germany prior to World War II. He was nurtured by the academic life of his father, Dr. Gerhart Niemeyer, and in his mother Lucie's home in South Bend, Indiana. He was educated at Indiana University and the University of Notre Dame. Prior to becoming a full-time photographer, he was the national sales manager of Volkswagen of America, and he later owned a VW dealership with his brother-in-law. An award-winning photographer, he has had one-man shows at the Museum of Natural History of the Smithsonian Institution in Washington, D.C., and in various galleries and museums in New York, New Jersey, Toronto, and Rio de Janeiro. He has photographed widely in Africa, the Caribbean, Europe, South America, and all regions of the United States, and his photographs have appeared in dozens of magazines, including *National Geographic Traveler*, *Life*, *Marie Claire*, *The World and I*, *Country Journal*, and *Travel and Holiday*. His books of photography include *Chesapeake Country* (Abbeville Press, 1990), *An African Perspective: A Portfolio of Selected Images* (LNS Arts, 1980), and *Long Legged Wading Birds of the North American Wetlands* (Stackpole Books, 1993). He is presently working on another book about Virginia's Shenandoah Valley. He lives in Aston, Pennsylvania, with his wife, Joan, and three children, Lucian, Michelle, and Heather.

Donald B. Kraybill was born into a Mennonite family and grew up on a dairy farm in Lancaster County, Pennsylvania. He received his B.A. from Eastern Mennonite College and his M.A. and Ph.D. from Temple University. He and his wife, Frances, have two daughters, Sheila and Joy. Widely recognized for his work on Anabaptist groups, Kraybill is the author of many books, among them *The Upside-Down Kingdom* (Herald Press, 1990), which received the National Religious Book Award; *The Riddle of Amish Culture* (Johns Hopkins University Press, 1989); *The Puzzles of Amish Life* (Good Books, 1990); and *The Amish and the State* (Johns Hopkins University Press, 1993), an edited collection. He is professor of sociology at Elizabethtown College (Pennsylvania), where he also directs the Young Center for the Study of Anabaptist and Pietist Goups.